ARK PAPERBACKS

THE SPIRIT IN MAN, ART AND LITERATURE

C.G. Jung (1875–1961), the Swiss psychiatrist and founder of Analytical Psychology, was an original thinker who made an immense contribution to the understanding of the human mind. In his early years he was a lecturer in psychiatry at the University of Zürich, and collaborated with Sigmund Freud. He gave up teaching to devote himself to his private practice in psychiatry and to research. He travelled widely and was a prolific author, often writing on subjects other than analytical psychology, such as mythology, alchemy, flying saucers, and the problem of time. Jung was also responsible for defining such influential and widely-used terms as the Collective Unconscious, Extraversion/Introversion, and Archetypes.

ARK

C.G. JUNG
THE SPIRIT
IN MAN, ART AND
LITERATURE

TRANSLATED BY R.F.C.HULL

ARK PAPERBACKS

First published in Great Britain in 1967

ARK Edition 1984

Reprinted 1989, 1993

ARK PAPERBACKS is an imprint of
Routledge
11 New Fetter Lane, London EC4P 4EE

Printed and bound in Great Britain by
Cox & Wyman Ltd, Reading

ISBN 0–7448–0008–0

EDITORIAL NOTE

There are different ways of looking at the achievements of out-standing personalities. Each can be studied in the light of his individual development, of the historical influences that played upon him, or of the more intangible collective influences expressed by the word *Zeitgeist*. Jung's attention was directed mainly to the great cultural movements—alchemy in particular —which compensated the *Zeitgeist* or arose from it, and to the creative spirit that introduced pioneering interpretations into realms as diverse as those of medicine, psychoanalysis, Oriental studies, the visual arts, and literature. The essays on Paracelsus, Freud, the sinologist Richard Wilhelm, Picasso, and Joyce's *Ulysses* have been brought together in illustration of this central theme; two others consider literary products independently of personality structure and the psychology of the individual artist. The source of scientific and artistic creativity in archetypal structures, and particularly in the dynamics of the "spirit archetype," forms an essential counterpoint to the theme underlying this collection of essays.

*

Grateful acknowledgment is made to those who helped in various ways to document and annotate the contents of this volume, particularly the essay on *Ulysses:* Leonard Albert, Daniel Brody, Ed. Bucher, Joseph Campbell, Stanley Dell, Richard Ellmann, Carola Giedion-Welcker, Stuart Gilbert, Jolande Jacobi, Aniela Jaffé, and Lilly Jung. For permission to quote from Joyce's *Ulysses* the publishers acknowledge to Random House, Inc., New York, and The Bodley Head Ltd., London.

TABLE OF CONTENTS

I V

V

I

PARACELSUS

PARACELSUS THE PHYSICIAN

PARACELSUS [1]

1   That remarkable man, Philippus Aureolus Bombast von Hohenheim, known as Theophrastus Paracelsus,[2] was born in this house on November 10, 1493. His medieval mind and questing spirit would not take it amiss if, in respectful remembrance of the customs of his day, we first glance at the position of the sun at the time of his birth. It stood in the sign of Scorpio, a sign that, according to ancient tradition, was favourable to physicians, the ministers of poisons and of healing. The ruler of Scorpio is the proud and bellicose Mars, who endows the strong with warlike courage and the weak with a quarrelsome and irascible disposition. The course of Paracelsus's life certainly did not belie his nativity.

2   Turning now from the heavens to the earth on which he was born, we see his parents' house embedded in a deep, lonely valley, darkly overhung by woods, and surrounded by the sombre towering mountains that shut in the moorlike slopes of the hills and declivities round about melancholy Einsiedeln. The great peaks of the Alps rise up menacingly close, the might of the earth visibly dwarfs the will of man; threateningly alive, it holds him fast in its hollows and forces its will upon him. Here, where nature is mightier than man, none escapes her influence; the chill of water, the starkness of rock, the gnarled, jutting roots of trees and precipitous cliffs—all this generates in the soul of anyone born there something that can never be extirpated, lending him that characteristically Swiss obstinacy, doggedness,

---

1 [An address delivered in the house in which Paracelsus was born, at Einsiedeln (Canton Schwyz), June, 1929, under the auspices of the Literary Club of Zurich, and published in *Der Lesezirkel* (Zurich), XVI:10 (Sept., 1929). Reprinted in *Wirklichkeit der Seele* (Zurich, 1934) and as a pamphlet (St. Gallen, 1952).—EDITORS.]

2 See the excellent edition of Paracelsus's writings prepared by Bernhard Aschner.

stolidity, and innate pride which have been interpreted in various ways—favourably as self-reliance, unfavourably as dour pighead-edness. "The Swiss are characterized by a noble spirit of liberty, but also by a certain coldness which is less agreeable," a French-man once wrote.

3   Father Sun and Mother Earth seem to have been more truly the begetters of his character than were Paracelsus's own beget-ters by blood. For, at any rate on his father's side, Paracelsus was not a Swiss but a Swabian, a son of Wilhelm Bombast, the ille-gitimate offspring of Georg Bombast of Hohenheim, Grand Master of the Order of the Knights of St. John. But, born under the spell of the Alps, in the lap of a more potent earth that, regardless of his blood, had made him her own, Paracelsus came into the world by character a Swiss, in accordance with the un-known topographical law that rules a man's disposition.

4   His mother came from Einsiedeln, and nothing is known of her influence. His father, on the other hand, was something of a problem. He had wandered into the country as a doctor and had settled down in that out-of-the-way spot along the pilgrims' route. What right had he, born illegitimate, to bear his father's noble name? One surmises the tragedy in the soul of the illegit-imate child: a grim, lonely man shorn of his birthright, nursing resentment against his homeland in the seclusion of his wooded valley, and yet, with unconfessed longing, receiving news from pilgrims of the world outside to which he will never return. Aristocratic living and the pleasures of cosmopolitanism were in his blood, and remained buried there. Nothing exerts a stronger psychic effect upon the human environment, and especially upon children, than the life which the parents have not lived. So we may expect this father to have exerted the most powerful influence on the young Paracelsus, who will have reacted in just the opposite way.

5   A great love—indeed, his only love—bound him to his father. This was the only man he remembered with love. A loyal son like this will make amends for his father's guilt. All the father's resignation will turn into consuming ambition in the son. The father's resentment and inevitable feelings of inferiority will make the son an avenger of his father's wrongs. He will wield his sword against all authority, and will do battle with everything

4

that lays claim to the *potestas patris,* as if it were his own father's adversary. What the father lost or had to relinquish—success, fame, a free-roving life in the great world—he will have to win back again. And, following a tragic law, he must also fall out with his friends, as the predestined consequence of the fateful bond with his only friend, his father—for psychic endogamy is attended by heavy punishments.

6   As is not uncommon, nature equipped him very badly for the role of avenger. Instead of an heroic figure fit for a rebel, she gave him a stature of a mere five feet, an unhealthy appearance, an upper lip that was too short and did not quite cover his teeth (often the distinguishing mark of nervous people), and, so it seems, a pelvis that struck everybody by its femininity when, in the nineteenth century, his bones were exhumed in Salzburg.[3] There is even a legend that he was a eunuch, though to my knowledge there is no further evidence of this. At all events, love seems never to have woven her roses into his earthly life, and he had no need of their thorns, since his character was prickly enough as it was.

7   Hardly had he reached an age to bear arms than the little man buckled on a sword much too big for him, from which he seldom let himself be parted, the less so because, in its ball-shaped pommel, he kept his laudanum pills, which were his true arcanum. Thus accoutred, a figure not entirely lacking in comedy, he set forth into the wide world on his amazing and hazardous journeys which took him to Germany, France, Italy, the Netherlands, Denmark, Sweden, and Russia. An eccentric thaumaturge, almost a second Apollonius of Tyana, he is supposed, according to legend, to have travelled to Africa and Asia, where he discovered the greatest secrets. He never undertook any regular studies, as submission to authority was taboo to him. He was a self-made man, who devised for himself the apt motto *Alterius non sit, qui suus esse potest,*[4] a right and proper Swiss sentiment. All that befell Paracelsus on his endless journeys must remain forever in the realm of conjecture, but probably it

---

[3] [Paracelsus died Sept. 24, 1541, at Salzburg, where he was buried in the cemetery of St. Sebastian, "among the poor of the almshouse" (Jacobi, in her edn. of Paracelsus' selected writings, p. lxi).—EDITORS.]
[4] "Let him not be another's who can be his own."

5

was a constant repetition of what happened to him in Basel. In 1525, already famed as a physician, he was summoned to Basel by the town council, the latter evidently acting in one of those rare fits of clear-headedness which now and then occur in the course of history, as the appointment of the youthful Nietzsche also shows. The appointment of Paracelsus had a somewhat distressing background, as Europe at that time was suffering under an unexampled epidemic of syphilis which had broken out after the Neapolitan campaign. Paracelsus occupied the post of a town physician, but he comported himself with a lack of dignity not at all to the taste of the university or of the worshipful public. He scandalized the former by giving his lectures in the language of stable-boys and scullions, that is, in German; the latter he outraged by appearing in the street, not in his robe of office, but in a labourer's jerkin. Among his colleagues he was the best-hated man in Basel, and not a hair was left unscathed in his medical treatises. He was known as the "mad bull," the "wild ass of Einsiedeln." He gave it all back, and more, in studiedly obscene invective, a far from edifying spectacle.

8   In Basel, fate dealt him a blow that struck deep into his life: he lost his friend and favourite pupil, the humanist Johannes Oporinus, who meanly betrayed him and supplied his enemies with the most powerful ammunition. Afterwards, Oporinus himself regretted his disloyalty, but it was too late; the damage could never be mended. Nothing, however, could dampen the arrogant and obstreperous behaviour of Paracelsus; on the contrary, the betrayal only increased it. He soon took to travelling again, mostly poverty-stricken and often reduced to beggary.

When he was thirty-eight, a characteristic change showed itself in his writings: philosophical treatises began to appear alongside his medical ones. "Philosophical" is hardly the right word for this spiritual phenomenon—one would do better to call it "Gnostic." This remarkable psychic change is one that usually occurs after the midpoint of life has been crossed, and it might be described as a reversal of the psychic current. Only rarely does this subtle change of direction appear clearly on the surface; in most people it takes place, like all the important things in life, beneath the threshold of consciousness. Among those with powerful minds, it manifests itself as a transformation of

6

the intellect into a kind of speculative or intuitive spirituality, as for instance in the case of Newton, Swedenborg, and Nietzsche. With Paracelsus, the tension between the opposites was not so marked, though it was noticeable enough.

9   This brings us, after having touched on the externals and the vicissitudes of his personal life, to Paracelsus the spiritual man, and we now enter a world of ideas that must seem extraordinarily dark and confusing to the man of the present, unless he has some special knowledge of the late-medieval mentality. Above all, Paracelsus—despite his high estimation of Luther—died a good Catholic, in strange contrast to his pagan philosophy. One can hardly suppose that Catholicism was simply his style of life. For him it was probably such a manifestly and completely incomprehensible thing that he never even reflected upon it, otherwise he would certainly have got into difficulties with the Church and with his own feelings. Paracelsus was evidently one of those people who keep their intellect and their feelings in different compartments, so that they can happily go on thinking with the intellect and not run the risk of colliding with what their feelings believe. It is indeed a great relief when the one hand does not know what the other is doing, and it would be idle curiosity to want to know what would happen if the two ever did collide. In those days, if all went well, they did not collide—this is the distinctive feature of that peculiar age, and it is quite as puzzling as the mentality, say, of Pope Alexander VI and of the whole higher clergy of the Cinquecento. Just as, in art, a merry paganism emerged from under the skirts of the Church, so, behind the curtain of scholastic disputation, a paganism of the spirit flourished in a rebirth of Neoplatonism and natural philosophy. Among the leaders of this movement it was particularly the Neoplatonism of the humanist Marsilio Ficino which influenced Paracelsus, as it did so many other aspiring "modern" minds in those days. Nothing is more characteristic of the explosive, revolutionary, futuristic spirit of the times, which left Protestantism far behind and anticipated the nineteenth century, than the motto of Agrippa von Nettesheim's book *De incertitudine et vanitate scientiarum* (1527):

> Nullis his parcet Agrippa,
> contemnit, scit, nescit, flet, ridet,

irascitur, insectatur, carpit omnia,
ipse philosophus, daemon, heros, deus et omnia.[5]

10   A new era had dawned, the overthrow of the authority of the Church was under way, and with it vanished the metaphysical certainty of the Gothic man. But whereas in Latin countries antiquity broke through in every conceivable form, the barbarous Germanic countries, instead of reverting to classical times, succumbed to the primitive experience of the spirit in all its immediacy, in different forms and at different levels, embodied by great and marvellous thinkers and poets like Meister Eckhart, Agrippa, Paracelsus, Angelus Silesius, and Jacob Boehme. All of them show their primitive but forceful originality by an impetuous language that has broken away from tradition and authority. Apart from Boehme, probably the worst rebel in this respect was Paracelsus. His philosophical terminology is so individual and so arbitrary that it surpasses by far the "power words" of the Gnostics in eccentricity and turgidity of style.

11   The highest cosmogonic principle, corresponding to the Gnostic demiurge, is the Yliaster or Hylaster, a hybrid compound of *hyle* (matter) and *astrum* (star). This concept might be translated as "cosmic matter." It is something like the "One" of Pythagoras and Empedocles, or the Heimarmene of the Stoics —a primitive conception of primary matter or energy. The Graeco-Latin coinage is no more than a fashionable stylistic flourish, a cultural veneer for a very ancient idea that had also fascinated the pre-Socratics, though there is no reason to suppose that Paracelsus inherited it from them. These archetypal images belong to humanity at large and can crop up autochthonously in anybody's head at any time and place, only needing favourable circumstances for their reappearance. The suitable moment for this is always when a particular view of the world is collapsing, sweeping away all the formulas that purported to offer final answers to the great problems of life. It is, as a matter of fact, quite in accord with psychological law that, when all the uprooted gods have come home to roost in man, he should cry out, "Ipse philosophus, daemon, heros, deus et omnia," and that, when a

[5] "Agrippa spares no man; he contemns, knows, knows not, weeps, laughs, waxes wroth, reviles, carps at all things; being himself philosopher, demon, hero, god, and all things."

religion glorifying the spirit disappears, there should rise up in its stead a primordial image of creative matter.

12 In strictest contrast to the Christian view, the supreme Paracelsan principle is thoroughly materialistic. The spiritual principle takes second place, this being the *anima mundi* that proceeds from matter, the "Ideos" or "Ides," the "Mysterium magnum" or "Limbus major, a spiritual being, an invisible and intangible thing." Everything is contained in it in the form of Plato's "eidola," the archetypes, a germinal idea that may have been implanted in Paracelsus by Marsilio Ficino. The "Limbus" is a circle. The animate world is the larger circle, man is the "Limbus minor," the smaller circle. He is the microcosm. Consequently, everything without is within, everything above is below. Between all things in the larger and smaller circles reigns "correspondence" (*correspondentia*), a notion that culminates in Swedenborg's *homo maximus* as a gigantic anthropomorphization of the universe. In the more primitive conception of Paracelsus the anthropomorphization is lacking. For him man and world alike are aggregates of animate matter, and this in turn is a notion that has an affinity with the scientific conceptions of the late nineteenth century, except that Paracelsus did not think mechanistically, in terms of inert, chemical matter, but in a primitive animistic way. For him nature swarmed with witches, incubi, succubi, devils, sylphs, undines, etc. The animation he experienced psychically was simultaneously the animation of nature. The death of all things psychic that took place in scientific materialism was still a long way off, but he prepared the ground for it. He was still an animist, in keeping with his primitive cast of mind, but already a materialist. Matter, as something infinitely distributed throughout space, is the absolute opposite of that concentration of the organic which is psyche. The world of sylphs and undines was soon to come to an end, and would be resurrected only in the psychological era, when one would wonder how such ancient truths could ever have been forgotten. But, of course, it is much simpler to suppose that what we do not understand does not exist.

13 The world of Paracelsus, macrocosmically and microcosmically, consisted of animate particles, or *entia*. Diseases, too, were *entia*, and in the same way there was an *ens astrorum, veneni, naturale, spirituale,* or *ideale*. The great epidemic of plague

9

raging at that time, he explained in a letter to the Emperor, was caused by succubi begotten in whore-houses. An *ens* was another "spiritual being," hence he said in his book *Paragranum:* "Diseases are not bodies, wherefore spirit must be used against spirit." By this he meant that, according to the doctrine of correspondence, for every *ens morbi* there existed a natural "arcanum" which could be used as a specific against the corresponding disease. For this reason he did not describe diseases clinically or anatomically, but in terms of their specifics; for instance, there were "tartaric" diseases, which could be cured by their specific *arcanum,* in this case tartar. Therefore he held in high esteem the doctrine of signatures, which seems to have been one of the main principles of folk-medicine in those days, as practised by midwives, army surgeons, witches, quacks, and hangmen. According to this doctrine, a plant, for instance, with leaves shaped like a hand is good for diseases of the hand, and so forth.

14   Disease for Paracelsus was "a natural growth, a spiritual, living thing, a seed." We may safely say that for him a disease was a proper and necessary constituent of life that lived together with man, and not a hated "alien body" as it is for us. It was kith and kin to the arcana which were present in nature and which, as nature's constituents, were as necessary to her as diseases were to man. Here the most modern doctor would shake Paracelsus by the hand and say: "I don't think it's quite like that, but it's not so far off." The whole world, said Paracelsus, was an apothecary's shop, and God the apothecary in chief.

15   Paracelsus had a mind typical of a crucial time of transition. His searching and wrestling intellect had broken free from a spiritual view of the world to which his feelings still clung. *Extra ecclesiam nulla salus*—this saying applies in the highest degree to every man whose spiritual transformation carries him beyond the magic circle of traditional holy images which, as ultimate truths, shut off the horizon: he loses all his comforting prejudices, his whole world falls apart, and he knows as yet nothing about a different order of things. He has become impoverished, as unknowing as a small child, still entirely ignorant of the new world, and able to recall only with difficulty the age-old experiences of mankind that speak to him from his blood. All

authority has dropped away, and he must build a new world out of his own experience.

16   On his long journeys Paracelsus gathered a rich harvest of experience, not scorning even the grimiest sources, for he was a pragmatist and empiricist without parallel. All this primary material he accepted without prejudice, at the same time drawing upon the primitive darkness of his own psyche for the philosophical ideas fundamental to his work. Old pagan beliefs, living on in the blackest superstitions of the populace, were fished up. Christian spirituality reverted to primitive animism, and out of this Paracelsus, with his scholastic training, concocted a philosophy that had no Christian prototype, but resembled far more the thinking of the most execrated enemies of the Church—the Gnostics. Like every ruthless innovator who rejects authority and tradition, he was in danger of retrogressing to the very things that they in turn had once rejected, and so reaching a lifeless and purely destructive standstill. But probably owing to the fact that, while his intellect roved far and wide and probed back into the distant past, his feelings still clung to the traditional values, the full consequences of retrogression were averted. Thanks to this unbearable opposition, regression turned into progression. He did not deny the spirit his feelings believed in, but erected beside it the counter-principle of matter: earth as opposed to heaven, nature as opposed to spirit. For this reason he was not a blind destroyer, a genius-*cum*-charlatan like Agrippa, but a father of natural science, a pioneer of the new spirit, and as such he is rightly honoured today. He would certainly shake his head at the idea for which some of his modern disciples most venerate him. His hard-won discovery was not "panpsychism"—this still clung to him as a relic of his primitive *participation mystique* with nature—but *matter and its qualities*. The conscious situation of his age and the existing state of knowledge did not allow him to see man outside the framework of nature as a whole. This was reserved for the nineteenth century. The indissoluble, unconscious oneness of man and world was still an absolute fact, but his intellect had begun to wrestle with it, using the tools of scientific empiricism. Modern medicine can no longer understand the psyche as a mere appendage of the body and is beginning to take the "psychic factor" more

and more into account. In this respect it approaches the Paracelsan conception of physically animated matter, with the result that the whole spiritual phenomenon of Paracelsus appears in a new light.

17   Just as Paracelsus was the great medical pioneer of his age, so today he is symbolic of an important change in our conception of the nature of disease and of life itself.

PARACELSUS THE PHYSICIAN [1]

18   Anyone who is at all familiar with the writings of that great
physician whose memory we honour today will know how impossible it is to give an adequate account in a lecture of all the
achievements that have made the name of Paracelsus immortal.
He was a veritable whirlwind, tearing up everything by the
roots and leaving behind him a pile of wreckage. Like an erupt-
ing volcano he laid waste and destroyed, but he also fertilized
and brought to life. It is impossible to be fair to him; one can
only underestimate him or overestimate him, and so one remains continually dissatisfied with one's own efforts to compre-
hend even one facet of his multitudinous nature. Even if one
limits oneself to sketching a picture of Paracelsus the "physician," one meets this physician on so many different levels and
in so many different guises that every attempt at portraiture remains a miserable patchwork. His prodigious literary output has
done little to clear up the general confusion, least of all the still
controversial question of the genuineness of some of the most
important writings, not to speak of the mass of contradictions
and arcane terms that make Paracelsus one of the greatest ob-
scurantists of the epoch. Everything about him was on an immense scale, or, we might equally well say, everything was exag-
gerated. Long dreary stretches of utter nonsense alternate with
oases of inspired insight, so rich and illuminating that one can-

1 [Originally delivered as a lecture to the Swiss Society for the History of Medi-
cine and the Natural Sciences, at the annual meeting of the Society for Nature
Research, Basel, Sept. 7, 1941, to commemorate the 400th anniversary of Paracelsus's death; published as "Paracelsus als Arzt," *Schweizerische medizinische
Wochenschrift* (Basel), LXXXI (1941): 40, 1153-70; republished in *Paracelsica:
Zwei Vorlesungen über den Arzt und Philosophen Theophrastus* (Zurich, 1942).
The other essay from *Paracelsica* is published in Vol. 13 of the *Coll. Works*
under the title "Paracelsus as a Spiritual Phenomenon," together with Jung's
foreword to *Paracelsica.*—EDITORS.]

.not shake off the uneasy feeling that somehow one has over-looked the main point of his argument.

19   Unfortunately, I cannot claim to be a Paracelsus specialist and to possess a full knowledge of the *Opera omnia*. If, for professional reasons, one has to devote oneself to other things than just Paracelsus, it is hardly possible to make a conscientious study of the two thousand six hundred folio pages of the Huser edition of 1616, or the still more comprehensive edition of Sudhoff. Paracelsus is an ocean, or, to put it less kindly, a chaos, an alchemical melting-pot into which the human beings, gods, and demons of that tremendous age, the first half of the sixteenth century, poured their peculiar juices. The first thing that strikes us on reading his works is his bilious and quarrelsome temperament. He raged against the academic physicians all along the line, and against their authorities, Galen, Avicenna, Rhazes, and the rest. The only exceptions (apart from Hippocrates) were the alchemical authorities, Hermes, Archelaos, Morienus, and others, whom he quotes with approval. In general, he attacked neither astrology[2] nor alchemy, nor any of the popular superstitions. On this latter account his works are a mine of information for the folklorist. There are only a few treatises from the pen of Paracelsus, except for theological ones, that do not reveal his fanatical hatred of academic medicine. Again and again one comes across violent outbursts that betray his bitterness and his personal grievances. It is quite clear that this was no longer objective criticism; it was the deposit of numerous personal disappointments that were especially bitter for him because he had no insight into his own faults. I mention this fact not in order to bring his personal psychology into the limelight, but to stress one of the chief impressions which his writings make on the reader. Practically every page bears in one way or another the human, often all too human stamp of this strange and powerful personality. His motto is said to have been *Alterius non sit, qui suus esse potest* (Let him not be another's who can be his own), and if this necessitated a ruthless, not to say brutal passion for independence, there is certainly no lack of literary as well as biographical proofs of its existence. As is the way of things, this rebellious defiance and harshness contrasted very strongly with

2 Not, at least, in principle. He did, however, expressly repudiate various superstitious abuses of astrology.

his loyal attachment to the Church and with the soft-heartedness and sympathy with which he treated his patients, particularly those who were destitute.

20   Paracelsus was both a conservative and a revolutionary. He was conservative as regards the basic truths of the Church, and of astrology and alchemy, but sceptical and rebellious, both in practice and theory, where academic medicine was concerned. It is largely to this that he owes his celebrity, for it seems to me very difficult to single out any medical discoveries *of a fundamental nature* that can be traced back to Paracelsus. What seems so important to us, the inclusion of surgery within the province of medicine, did not, for Paracelsus, mean developing a new science, but merely taking over the arts of the barbers and field-surgeons along with those of midwives, witches, sorcerers, astrologers, and alchemists. I feel I ought to apologize for the heretical thought that, if Paracelsus were alive today, he would undoubtedly be the advocate of all those arts which academic medicine prevents us from taking seriously, such as osteopathy, magnetopathy, iridodiagnosis, faith-healing, dietary manias, etc. If we imagine for a moment the emotions of faculty members at a modern university where there were professors of iridodiagnosis, magnetopathy, and Christian Science, we can understand the outraged feelings of the medical faculty at Basel when Paracelsus burned the classic text-books of medicine, gave his lectures in German, and, scorning the dignified gown of the doctor, paraded the streets in a workman's smock. The glorious Basel career of the "wild ass of Einsiedeln," as he was called, came to a speedy end. The impish impedimenta of the Paracelsan spirit were a bit too much for the respectable doctors of his day.

21   In this respect we have the valuable testimony of a medical contemporary, the learned Dr. Conrad Gessner, of Zurich, in the form of a letter, written in Latin, to Ferdinand I's personal physician, Crato von Crafftheim, dated August 16, 1561.[3] Although written twenty years after the death of Paracelsus, it is still redolent of the reactions he provoked. Replying to a question of Crato's, Gessner states that he had no list of Paracelsus's writings, nor would he bother to get one, since he considered Theophrastus utterly unworthy to be mentioned along with re-

3 *Epistolarum Conradi Gessneri, Philosophici Medici Tiguri, Libri III* (Zurich, 1577), fol. 2v-r.

spectable authors, let alone with Christian ones, and certainly not with pious citizens, such as even the pagans were. He and his followers were nothing but Arian heretics. He had been a sorcerer and had intercourse with demons. "The Basel Carolostadius," continues Gessner, "by name of Bodenstein,[4] a few months ago sent a treatise of Theophrastus, 'De anatome corporis humani,' here to be printed. In it he makes mock of physicians who examine single parts of the body and carefully determine their position, shape, number, and nature, but neglect the most important thing, namely, to what stars and to what regions of the heavens each part belongs."

22   Gessner ends with the lapidary words: "But our typographers have refused to print it." The letter tells us that Paracelsus was not counted among the "boni scriptores." He was even suspected of practising divers kinds of magic and—worse still—of the Arian heresy.[5] Both these were capital offences at that time. Such accusations may do something to explain the restlessness of Paracelsus and his wanderlust, which never left him and drove him from city to city through half Europe. He may very well have been concerned for his skin. Gessner's attack on "De anatome corporis humani" is justified in so far as Paracelsus really did make mock of anatomical dissection, then beginning to be practised, because he said the doctors saw nothing at all in the cut-up organs. He himself was mainly interested in the cosmic correlations, such as he found in the astrological tradition. His doctrine of the "star in the body" was a favourite idea of his, and it occurs everywhere in his writings. True to the conception of man as a microcosm, he located the "firmament" in man's body and called it the "astrum" or "Sydus." It was an endosomatic heaven, whose constellations did not coincide with the astronomical heaven but originated with the individual's nativity, the "ascendant" or horoscope.

23   Gessner's letter shows how Paracelsus was judged by a contemporary colleague, and an authoritative one at that. We must now try to get a picture of Paracelsus as a physician from his own writings. For this purpose I shall let the Master speak in his own

4 Adam von Bodenstein, editor of the *Vita longa* and a pupil of Paracelsus in Basel.
5 Paracelsus himself mentions the accusation in "Haeresiarcha." Cf. *Das Buch Paragranum*, ed. Strunz, preface, p. 18.

words, but since these words contain a good many that he made up himself, I must now and then interject a comment.

24   Part of the doctor's function is to be equipped with special knowledge. Paracelsus is also of this opinion, though with the strange qualification that a "made" doctor has to be a hundred times more industrious than a "natural" one, because everything comes to the latter from the "light of nature." He himself, it seems, studied at Ferrara and obtained his doctor's degree there. He also acquired knowledge of the classical medicine of Hippocrates, Galen, and Avicenna, having already received some kind of preliminary education from his father. Let us hear, from the *Book Paragranum*,[6] what he has to say about the physician's art:

> What then is the physician's art? He should know what is useful and what harmful to intangible things, to the *beluis marinis,* to the fishes, what is pleasant and unpleasant, healthy and unhealthy to the beasts: these are the arts relating to natural things. What more? The wound-blessings and their powers, why and for what cause they do what they do: what *Melosina* is, and what *Syrena,* what *permutatio, transplantatio* and *transmutatio* are, and how they may be fully understood: what is above nature, what is above species, what is above life, what the visible is and the invisible, what produces sweetness and bitterness, what taste is, what death is, what is useful to fishermen, what a currier, a tanner, a dyer, a blacksmith, and a carpenter should know, what belongs in the kitchen, in the cellar, in the garden, what belongs to time, what a hunter knows, what a mountaineer knows, what befits a traveller, what befits a sedentary man, what warfare requires, what makes peace, what makes clerics and laymen, what every calling does, what every calling is, what God is, what Satan, what poison, and what the antidote to poison is, what there is in women, what in men, what distinguishes women from maidens, yellow from white, white from black, and red from fallow, in all things, why one colour here, another there, why short, why long, why success, why failure: and wherein this knowledge applies to all things.

25   This quotation introduces us straight away to the strange sources of Paracelsus's empiricism. We see him as a wandering scholar on the road, with a company of travellers; he turns in at

---

[6] Ibid., p. 105. [For the translation of the quotations from Paracelsus I am greatly indebted to Dr. R. T. Llewellyn.—TRANS.]

the village smith, who, as the chief medical authority, knows all the spells for healing wounds and stanching blood. From hunters and fishermen he hears wondrous tales of land and water creatures; of the Spanish tree-goose, which on putrefying turns into tortoises, or of the fertilizing power of the wind in Portugal, which begets mice in a sheaf of straw set up on a pole.[7] The ferryman tells of the *Lorind,* which causes the mysterious "crying and echoing of the waters." [8] Animals sicken and cure themselves like people, and the mountain folk even tell of the diseases of metals, of the leprosy of copper, and such things.[9] All this the physician should know. He should also know of the wonders of nature and the strange correspondence of the microcosm with the macrocosm, and not only with the visible universe, but with the invisible cosmic arcana, the mysteries. We meet one of these arcana at once—Melusina, a magical creature belonging half to folklore and half to the alchemical doctrine of Paracelsus, as her connection with the *permutatio* and *transmutatio* shows. According to him, Melusines dwell in the blood, and, since blood is the ancient seat of the soul, we may conjecture that Melusina is a kind of *anima vegetativa.* She is, in essence, a variant of the mercurial spirit, which in the fourteenth and fifteenth centuries was depicted as a female monster. Unfortunately, I must refrain from going into this figure more closely, as it would lead us into the depths of alchemical speculation.

26   But now let us return to our theme—the physician's science, as Paracelsus conceives it. The *Book Paragranum* says that the physician "sees and knows all disease outside the human body," [10] and that "the physician should proceed from external things, not from man." [11] "Therefore the physician proceeds from what is before his eyes, and from what is before him he sees what is behind him, that is: from the external he sees the internal. Only external things give knowledge of the internal; without them no internal thing may be known." [12] This means that the physician gains his knowledge of disease less from the sick

---

[7] *Liber Azoth,* ed. Huser, pp. 534 and 535. He declares that he witnessed the transformation of the tree-goose himself.

[8] *De caducis* (Huser, I), p. 595.

[9] *Paragranum.* The *leprositas aeris* is a well-known idea in alchemy. Cf. *Faust II:* "It's only rust that gives the coin its worth."

[10] P. 33.   [11] P. 39.   [12] P. 53.

person than from other natural phenomena that apparently have nothing to do with man, and above all from alchemy. "If they do not know that," says Paracelsus, "then they do not know the *Arcana*. And if they do not know what makes copper and what engenders the *Vitriolata*, then they do not know what causes leprosy. And if they do not know what makes rust on iron, then they do not know what causes ulcerations. And if they do not know what makes earthquakes, then they do not know what causes cold ague. External things teach and reveal the causes of man's infirmities, and man does not reveal the infirmity himself." [13]

27   Evidently, then, the physician recognizes from, say, the diseases of the metals what disease a man is suffering from. He must in any case be an alchemist. He "must employ the *Scientia Alchimiae* and not the foul brew of the Montpellier school," which is "such filthy hogwash that even the pigs would rather eat offal." [14] He must know the health and diseases of the elements. [15] As the *"species lignorum, lapidum, herbarum"* are likewise in man, he must know them too. Gold, for example, is a "natural comfortative" in man. [16] There is an "external art of Alchemy," but also an "Alchimia microcosmi," and the digestive process is such. The stomach, according to Paracelsus, is the alchemist in the belly. The physician must know alchemy in order to make his medicines, in particular the arcana such as *aurum potabile*, the *tinctura Rebis*, the *tinctura procedens*, the *Elixir tincturae*, and the rest. [17] Here, as so often, Paracelsus makes mock of himself, for he "knows not how," yet he says of the academic physicians: "You all talk drivel and have made yourselves strange dictionaries and vocabularies. No one can look at them without being led by the nose, and yet people are sent to the apothecary's with this incomprehensible jargon when they have better medicine in their own garden." [18] The arcana play a great role in Paracelsan therapy, especially in the treatment of mental diseases. "For in the *Arcanis*," says Paracelsus, "the tuff-stone becomes jacinth, the liver-stone alabaster, the flint garnet, clay a noble bolus, sand pearls, nettles manna, *Ungula* balsam. Herein lies the description of things, and in

[13] P. 35.   [14] *Labyrinthus medicorum errantium* (Huser, I), p. 272.
[15] Ibid., p. 269.   [16] P. 270.
[17] *De morbis amentium*, Part II, ch. VI (Huser, I), p. 506.   [18] *Paragranum*, p. 32.

these things the physician should be well grounded." [19] And in conclusion Paracelsus cries out: "Is it not true that Pliny never proved anything? Then what did he write? What he heard from the alchemists. If you do not know these things and what they are, you are a quack!" Thus the physician must know alchemy in order to diagnose human diseases from their analogy with the diseases of minerals. And finally, he himself is the subject of the alchemical process of transformation, since he is "ripened" by it.[20]

28   This difficult remark refers once more to the secret doctrine. Alchemy was not simply a chemical procedure as we understand it, but far more a philosophical procedure, a special kind of yoga, in so far as yoga also seeks to bring about a psychic transformation. For this reason the alchemists drew parallels between their *transmutatio* and the transformation symbolism of the Church.

29   The physician had to be not only an alchemist but also an astrologer,[21] for a second source of knowledge was the "firmament." In his *Labyrinthus medicorum* Paracelsus says that the stars in heaven must be "coupled together," and that the physician must "extract the judgment of the firmament from them." [22] Lacking this art of astrological interpretation, the physician is but a "pseudomedicus." The firmament is not merely the cosmic heaven, but a body which is a part or content of the human body. "Where the body is, there will the eagles gather. And where the medicine is, there do the physicians gather." [23] The firmamental body is the corporeal equivalent of the astrological heaven.[24] And since the astrological constellation makes a diagnosis possible, it also indicates the therapy. In this sense the firmament may be said to contain the "medicine." The physicians gather round the firmamental body like eagles round a carcass because, as Paracelsus says in a not very savoury comparison, "the carcass of the natural light" lies in the firmament. In other words, the *corpus sydereum* is the source of illumination by the *lumen naturae,* the "natural light," which plays

[19] Ibid., pp. 65f.   [20] Pp. 80, 83.
[21] Paracelsus makes no real distinction between astronomy and astrology.
[22] Ch. II (Huser, I), p. 267.   [23] Ibid.
[24] *Paragranum*, p. 50: "As in the heavens so also in the body the stars float free, pure, and have an invisible influence, like the arcana."

the greatest possible role not only in the writings of Paracelsus but in the whole of his thought. This intuitive conception is, in my opinion, an achievement of the utmost historical importance, for which no one should grudge Paracelsus undying fame. It had a great influence on his contemporaries and an even greater one on the mystic thinkers who came afterwards, but its significance for philosophy in general and for the theory of knowledge in particular still lies dormant. Its full development is reserved for the future.

30   The physician should learn to know this inner heaven. "For if he knows heaven only externally, he remains an astronomer and an astrologer; but if he establishes its order in man, then he knows two heavens. Now these two give the physician knowledge of the part which the upper sphere influences. This [part?] must be present without infirmity in the physician in order that he may know the *Caudam Draconis* in man, and know the *Arietem* and *Axem Polarem,* and his *Lineam Meridionalem,* his Orient and his Occident." "From the external we learn to know the internal." "Thus there is in man a firmament as in heaven, but not of one piece; there are two. For the hand that divided light from darkness, and the hand that made heaven and earth, has done likewise in the microcosm below, having taken from above and enclosed within man's skin everything that heaven contains. For that reason the external heaven is a guide to the heaven within. Who, then, will be a physician who does not know the external heaven? For we live in this same heaven and it lies before our eyes, whereas the heaven within us is not before the eyes but behind them, and therefore we cannot see it. For who can see through the skin? No one." [25]

31   We are involuntarily reminded of Kant's "starry heaven above me" and "moral law within me"—that "categorical imperative" which, psychologically speaking, took the place of the Heimarmene (compulsion of the stars) of the Stoics. There can be no doubt that Paracelsus was influenced by the Hermetic idea of "heaven above, heaven below." [26] In his conception of the inner heaven he glimpsed an eternal primordial image,

[25] Ibid., p. 52.
[26] Paracelsus certainly knew the "Tabula smaragdina," the classical authority of medieval alchemy, and the text: "What is below is like what is above. What is above is like what is below. Thus is the miracle of the One accomplished."

which was implanted in him and in all men, and recurs at all times and places. "In every human being," he says, "there is a special heaven, whole and unbroken." [27] "For a child which is being conceived already has its heaven." "As the great heaven stands, so it is imprinted at birth." [28] Man has "his Father in heaven and also in the air, he is a child that is made and born from the air and from the firmament." There is a "linea lactea" in heaven and in us. "The galaxa goes through the belly." [29] The poles and the zodiac are likewise in the human body. "It is necessary," he says, "that a physician should recognize the ascendants, the conjunctions, the exaltations, etc., of the planets, and that he understand and know all the constellations. And if he knows these things externally in the Father, it follows that he will know them in man, even though the number of men is so very great, and where to find heaven with its concordance in everyone, where health, where sickness, where beginning, where end, where death. For heaven is man and man is heaven, and all men are one heaven, and heaven is only one man." [30] The "Father in heaven" is the starry heaven itself. Heaven is the *homo maximus,* and the *corpus sydereum* is the representative of the *homo maximus* in the individual. "Now man was not born of man, for the first man had no progenitor, but was created. From created matter there grew the *Limbus,* and from the *Limbus* man was created and man has remained of the *Limbus.* And since he has remained so, he must be apprehended through the Father and not from himself, because he is enclosed in the skin (and no one can see through this and the workings within him are not visible). For the external heaven and the heaven within him are one, but in two parts. Even as Father and Son are two [aspects of one Godhead], so there is one Anatomy [which has

---

[27] *Paragranum,* p. 56.   [28] Ibid., p. 57.

[29] P. 48. Cf. the description in "De ente astrali," *Fragmenta ad Paramirum* (Huser, I, p. 132): "The heavens are a spirit and a vapour in which we live just like a bird in time. Not only the stars or the moon etc. constitute the heavens, but also there are stars in us, and these which are in us and which we do not see constitute the heavens also . . . the firmament is twofold, that of the heavens and that of the bodies, and these latter agree with each other, and not the body with the firmament . . . man's strength comes from the upper firmament and all his power lies in it. As the former may be weak or strong, so, too, is the firmament in the body . . ."   [30] *Paragranum,* p. 56.

two aspects]. Whoever knows the one, will also know the other." [31]

32   The heavenly Father, the *homo maximus,* can also fall sick, and this enables the physician to make his human diagnoses and prognoses. Heaven, says Paracelsus, is its own physician, "as the dog of its wounds." But man is not. Therefore he must "seek the locus of all sickness and health in the Father, and be mindful that this organ is of Mars, this of Venus, this of Luna," etc.[32] This evidently means that the physician has to diagnose sickness and health from the condition of the Father, or heaven. The stars are important aetiological factors. "Now all infection starts in the stars, and from the stars it follows afterwards in man. That is to say, if heaven is for it, then it begins in man. Now heaven does not enter into man—we should not talk nonsense on that account—but the stars in man, as ordered by God's hand, copy what heaven starts and brings to birth externally, and therefore it follows in man. It is like the sun shining through a glass and the moon giving light on the earth: but this does not injure a man, corrupting his body and causing diseases. For no more than the sun itself comes down to the earth do the stars enter a man, and their rays give a man nothing. The *Corpora* must do that and not the rays, and these are the *Corpora Microcosmi Astrali,* which gives the nature of the Father." [33] The *Corpora Astrali* are the same as the aforementioned *corpus sydereum* or *astrale.* Elsewhere Paracelsus says that "diseases come from the Father" [34] and not from man, just as the woodworm does not come from the wood.

33   The *astrum* in man is important not only for diagnosis and prognosis, but also for therapy. "From this emerges the reason why heaven is unfavourable to you and will not guide your medicine, so that you accomplish nothing: heaven must guide it for you. And the art lies, therefore, in that very place [i.e., heaven]. Say not that Melissa is good for the womb, or Marjoram for the head: so speak the ignorant. Such matters lie in Venus and in Luna, and if you wish them to have the effect you claim, you must have a favourable heaven or there will be no effect. Therein lies the error that has become prevalent in medicine:

[31] P. 55.   [32] P. 60.   [33] P. 54.   [34] P. 48.

23

Just hand out remedies, if they work, they work. Any peasant lad can engage in such practices, it takes no Avicenna or Galen." [35] When the physician has brought the *corpus astrale*, that is, the physiological Saturn (spleen) or Jupiter (liver), into the right connection with heaven, then, says Paracelsus, he is "on the right road." "And he should know, accordingly, how to make the Astral Mars and the physical Mars [the *corpus astrale*] subservient to one another, and how to conjugate and unite them. For this is the core which no physician from the first until myself has bit into. Thus it is understood that the medicine must be prepared in the stars and become firmamental. For the upper stars bring sickness and death, and also make well. Now if anything is to be done, it cannot be done without the *Astra*. And if it is to be done with the *Astra,* then the preparation should be completed at the same time as the medicine is being made and prepared by heaven." [36] The physician must "recognize the kind of medicine according to the stars and that, therefore, there are *Astra* both above and below. And since medicine can do nothing without heaven, it must be guided by heaven." This means that the astral influence must direct the alchemical procedure and the preparation of arcane remedies. "The course of heaven teaches the course and regimen of the fire in the Athanar.[37] For the virtue which lies in the sapphire comes from heaven by means of solution and coagulation and fixation." [38] Of the practical use of medicines Paracelsus says: "Medicine is in the will of the stars and is guided and directed by the stars. What belongs to the brain is directed to the brain by Luna; what belongs to the spleen is directed to the spleen by Saturn; what belongs to the heart is directed to the heart by Sol; and similarly to the kidneys by Venus, to the liver by Jupiter, to the bile by Mars. And not only is this so with these [organs], but with all the others which cannot be mentioned here." [39]

34   The names of diseases should likewise be correlated with astrology, and so should anatomy, which for Paracelsus meant nothing less than the astrophysiological structure of man, a "concordance with the machine of the world," and nothing at all resembling what Vesalius understood by it. It was not enough to cut open the body, "like a peasant looking at a psal-

[35] P. 73.   [36] P. 72.   [37] Alchemical furnace.
[38] *Paragranum*, p. 77.   [39] P. 73.

ter." [40] For him anatomy meant something like analysis. Accordingly he says: "Magic is the *Anatomia Medicinae*. Magic divides up the *corpora* of medicine." [41] But anatomy was also a kind of re-remembering of the original knowledge inborn in man, which is revealed to him by the *lumen naturae*. In his *Labyrinthus medicorum* he says: "How much labour and toil did the Mille Artifex[42] need to wrest this Anatomy from out the memory of man, to make him forget this noble art and lead him into vain imaginings and other mischief wherein there is no art, and which consume his time on earth unprofitably! For he who knows nothing loves nothing . . . but he who understands loves, observes, sees." [43]

35   With regard to the names of diseases, Paracelsus thought they should be chosen according to the zodiac and the planets, e.g., *Morbus leonis, sagittarii, martis,* etc. But he himself seldom adhered to this rule. Very often he forgot how he had called something and then invented a new name for it—which, incidentally, only adds to our difficulties in trying to understand his writings.

36   We see, therefore, that for Paracelsus aetiology, diagnosis, prognosis, therapy, nosology, pharmacology, pharmaceutics, and —last but not least—the daily hazards of medical practice were all directly related to astrology. Thus he admonished his colleagues: "You should see to it, all you physicians, that you know the cause of fortune and misfortune: until you can do this, keep away from medicine." [44] This could mean that if the indications elicited from the patient's horoscope were unfavourable, the doctor had an opportunity to make himself scarce—a very welcome one in those robust times, as we also know from the career of the great Dr. Cardan.

37   But not content with being an alchemist and astrologer, the physician had also to be a philosopher. What did Paracelsus mean by "philosophy"? Philosophy, as he understood it, had nothing whatever to do with our conception of the matter. For him it was something "occult," as we would say. We must not forget that Paracelsus was an alchemist through and through, and that the "natural philosophy" he practised had far less to do with thinking than with *experience*. In the alchemical tradition

[40] *Lab. med.,* ch. IV (Huser, I), p. 270.   [41] Ibid., ch. IX, p. 277.   [42] The devil.
[43] *Lab. med.,* ch. IX, p. 278.   [44] *Paragranum,* p. 67.

"philosophia," "sapientia," and "scientia" were essentially the same. Although they were treated as abstract ideas, they were in some strange way imagined as being quasi-material, or at least as being contained in matter,[45] and were designated accordingly. Hence they appeared in the form of quicksilver or Mercurius, lead or Saturn, gold or *aurum non vulgi*, salt or *sal sapientiae*, water or *aqua permanens*, etc. These substances were arcana, and like them philosophy too was an arcanum. In practice, this meant that philosophy was as it were concealed in matter and could also be found there.[46] We are obviously dealing with psychological projections, that is, with a primitive state of mind still very much in evidence at the time of Paracelsus, the chief symptom of which is the unconscious identity of subject and object.

38   These preparatory remarks may help us to understand Paracelsus's question: "What is nature other than philosophy?"[47] "Philosophy" was in man and outside him. It was like a mirror, and this mirror consisted of the four elements, for in the elements the microcosm was reflected.[48] The microcosm could be known from its "mother,"[49] i.e., elemental "matter." There were really two "philosophies," relating respectively to the lower and higher spheres. The lower philosophy had to do with minerals, the higher with the *Astra*.[50] By this he meant astronomy, from which we can see how thin was the dividing line between philosophy and "Scientia." This is made very clear when we are told that philosophy was concerned with earth and water, as-

[45] Hence the alchemists' strange but characteristic use of language, as for instance: "That body is the place of the science, gathering it together," etc. (Mylius, *Philosophia reformata*, p. 123.)

[46] The "Liber quartorum" (10th cent.) speaks of the *extraction of thought*. The relevant passage runs: "Those seated by the river Euphrates are the Chaldaeans, who are skilled in the stars and in judging them, and they were the first to accomplish the extraction of thought." These inhabitants of the banks of the Euphrates were probably the Sabaeans or Harranites, to whose learned activities we owe the transmission of a great many scientific treatises of Alexandrian origin. Here, as in Paracelsus, alchemical transformation is connected with the influence of the stars. The same passage says: "They who sit by the banks of the Euphrates convert gross bodies into a simple appearance, with the help of the movement of the higher bodies" (*Theatrum chemicum*, 1622, V, p. 144). Compare the "extraction of thought" with the Paracelsan saying that the Archasius "attracts science and prudence." See infra, par. 39.

[47] *Paragranum*, p. 26.   [48] Ibid., p. 27.   [49] Pp. 28, 29.   [50] Pp. 13, 33.

tronomy with air and fire.[51] Like philosophy, Scientia was in-born in all creatures; thus the pear-tree produced pears only by virtue of its Scientia. Scientia was an "influence" hidden in na-ture, and one needed "magic" in order to reveal this arcanum. "All else is vain delusion and madness, from which are begotten the fantasts." The gift of Scientia had to be "raised alchemically to the highest pitch," [52] that is to say it had to be distilled, sub-limated, and subtilized like a chemical substance. If the "Scien-tiae of nature" are not in the physician, "you will only hem and haw and know nothing for certain but the babbling of your mouth." [53]

39   So it is not surprising that philosophy also involved practical work. "In philosophy is knowledge, the entire globulus, and this by means of the *practica*. For philosophy is nothing other than the *practica globuli* or *sphaerae*. . . . Philosophy teaches the powers and properties of earthly and watery things . . . there-fore concerning philosophy I will tell you that just as there is in the earth a philosopher, so is there also in man, for one philoso-pher is of the earth, another of water," etc.[54] Thus there is a "philosopher" in man just as there is an "alchemist," who, we have heard, is the stomach. This same philosophizing function is also found in the earth and can be "extracted" from it. The "practica globuli" mentioned in the text means the alchemical treatment of the *massa globosa* or *prima materia,* the arcane sub-stance; hence philosophy was in essence an alchemical proce-dure.[55] For Paracelsus, philosophical cognition was actually an activity of the object itself, therefore he calls it a "Zuwerffen": the object "throws" its meaning at man. "The tree . . . gives the name tree without [the aid of] the alphabet"; it says what it is and contains, just as the stars do, which have within them their own "firmamental judgment." Thus Paracelsus can assert that it is the "Archasius" [56] in man which "draws to itself

[51] P. 47.   [52] *Lab. med.*, ch. VI (Huser, I), p. 273.   [53] Ibid.

[54] *Fragmenta medica*, Lib. IV Columnarum Medicinae (Huser, I), p. 142.

[55] In this respect, too, Paracelsus showed himself to be a conservative alchemist, for even in antiquity the fourfold alchemical procedure was known as τετρα-μερεῖν τὴν φιλοσοφίαν, "the division of the philosophy into four parts" (Berthelot, *Alch. grecs*, III, xliv, 5).

[56] "Archasius" is probably the same as "Archeus," the life-warmth, also called Vulcan. It seems to have been localized in the belly, where it took care of digestion and produced "foods," just as the *archeus terrae* produced metals.

scientiam atque prudentiam." [57] Indeed, he admits with great humility: "What does man invent out of himself or through himself? Not enough to patch a pair of breeches with." [58] Besides which not a few of the medical arts are "revealed by devils and spirits." [59]

40   I won't pile up quotations, but from all this it should be clear that the physician's "philosophy" was of an arcane nature. That Paracelsus was a great admirer of magic and the *Ars cabbalistica,* the "Gabal," is only to be expected. If a physician does not know magic, he says, he is a "well-intentioned madman in medicine, who inclines more to deception than to the truth." Magic is a preceptor and teacher.[60] Accordingly, Paracelsus made many amulets and seals,[61] so it was partly his own fault if he got a bad reputation for practising magic. Speaking of physicians in times to come—and this peering into the future is characteristic—he says: "They will be *Geomantici,* they will be *Adepti,* they will be *Archei,* they will be *Spagyri,* they will possess the *Quintum esse."* [62] The chemical dream of alchemy has been fulfilled, and it was Paracelsus who foresaw the role which chemistry was destined to play in present-day medicine.

41   Before I bring my all too summary remarks to a close, I would like to lay stress on one highly important aspect of his therapy, namely, the psychotherapeutic aspect. Paracelsus still practised the ancient art of "charming" an illness, of which the Ebers Papyrus gives so many excellent examples from ancient Egypt.[63] Paracelsus calls this method *Theorica.* He concedes that there is a *Theorica Essentiae Curae* and a *Theorica Essentiae Causae,* but immediately adds that the *"Theorica curae et*

This was the alchemist of the earth who regulated the "mineral fire in the mountains" *(De transmutationibus rerum naturalium,* Lib. VII, Huser, I, p. 900). We find this idea also in the "Liber quartorum," where the Archeus is called "Alkian" or "Alkien." "Alkian is . . . the spirit that nourishes and governs man, through which comes about the conversion of his food and his animal generation, and through it man exists" *(Theatr. chem.,* 1622, V, p. 152). "The Alkien of the earth is the animal Alkien: at the ends of the earth . . . are powers . . . like those animal powers which the physicians call Alkien" (ibid., p. 191).

57 *De vita longa,* Lib. I, ch. IX, ed. Bodenstein, p. 26.   58 *Paragranum,* p. 98.
59 *Von dem Podagra* (Huser, I), p. 541.   60 *Lab. med.,* ch. IX (Huser, I), p. 277.
61 *Archidoxis magicae,* Lib. I (Huser, II), p. 546.   62 *Paragranum,* preface, p. 21.
63 G. Ebers, *Papyros E. Das hermetische Buch über die Arzneimittel der alten Aegypter.*

causae are hidden together and inseparably one." What the physician has to say to the patient will depend on his own nature: "He must be whole and complete, otherwise he will discover nothing." The light of nature must give him instruction, that is, he must proceed intuitively, for only by illumination can he understand "nature's textbooks." The "theoricus medicus" must therefore speak with God's mouth, for the physician and his medicines were created by God,[64] and just as the theologian draws his truth from the holy revealed scripture, the physician draws it from the light of nature. The *Theorica* is a "religio medici." He gives an example of how it should be practised and how to speak to the patient: "Or a dropsical patient says his liver is chilled, etc., and consequently they are inclined to dropsy. Such reasons are much too trivial. But if you say the cause is a meteoric semen which turns to rain, and the rain percolates down from above, from the *media interstitia* into the lower parts, so that the semen becomes a stretch of water, a pond, a lake, then you have put your finger on it. It is like when you see a fine, clear cloudless sky: suddenly a little cloud appears, which grows and increases, so that within an hour a great rain, hailstorm, shower, etc., sets in. This is how we should theorize concerning the fundamentals of medicine in disease, as has been said."[65] One can see how suggestively this must have worked on the patient: the meteorological comparison induces a precipitation, immediately the sluices of the body open and the ascites stream off. Even in organic diseases such psychic stimulation is not to be underestimated, and I am convinced that more than one of the miraculous cures of the Master can be traced back to his admirable *theorica*.

42   Concerning the physician's attitude to the patient, Paracelsus has many good things to say. From the wealth of utterances on this subject I would like, in conclusion, to quote a few scattered sayings from the *Liber de caducis*.[66] "First of all it is very necessary to tell of the compassion that must be innate in a physician." "Where there is no love, there is no art." Physician and medicine "are both nothing other than a mercy conferred on the needy by God." The art is achieved by the "work of

---

[64] God loves the physician above all scholars. Therefore he should be truthful and not a "man of masks" (*Paragranum*, p. 95).

[65] *Lab. med.*, ch. VIII (Huser, I), p. 276.   [66] Huser, I, p. 589ff.

love." "Thus the physician must be endowed with no less compassion and love than God intends towards man." Compassion is "the physician's mentor." "I under the Lord, the Lord under me, I under Him outside my office, He under me outside His office. Thus each is subordinate to the other's office, and in such love each subordinate to the other." What the physician does is not *his* work: he is "the means by which nature is put to work." Medicine "grows unbidden and pushes up from the earth even if we sow nothing." "The practice of this art lies in the heart: if your heart is false, the physician within you will be false." "Let him not say with desperate Satan: it is impossible." He should put his trust in God. "For sooner will the herbs and roots speak with you, and in them will be the power you need." "The physician has partaken of the banquet to which the invited guests did not come."

43   With this I come to the end of my lecture. I shall be content if I have succeeded in giving you at least a few impressions of the strange personality and the spiritual force of the celebrated physician whom his contemporaries rightly named the "Luther of medicine." Paracelsus was one of the great figures of the Renaissance, and one of the most unfathomable. For us he is still an enigma, four hundred years afterwards.

II

FREUD IN HIS HISTORICAL SETTING

IN MEMORY OF SIGMUND FREUD

SIGMUND FREUD IN HIS HISTORICAL SETTING [1]

44   It is always a delicate and dangerous task to place a living man in historical perspective. But at least it is possible to gauge his significance and the extent to which he has been conditioned by history if his life-work and system of thought form a self-contained whole as do Freud's. His teaching, which in its fundamentals is probably known to every educated layman today, is not limitless in its ramifications, nor does it include any extraneous elements whose origins lie in other fields of science; it is based on a few transparent principles which, to the exclusion of everything else, dominate and permeate the whole substance of his thought. The originator of this teaching has, moreover, identified it with his method of "psychoanalysis," thereby making it into a rigid system that may rightly be charged with absolutism. On the other hand, the extraordinary emphasis laid upon this theory causes it to stand out as a strange and unique phenomenon against its philosophical and scientific background. Nowhere does it merge with other contemporary concepts, nor has its author made any conscious effort to connect it with its historical predecessors. This impression of isolation is heightened still further by a peculiar terminology which at times borders on subjective jargon. To all appearances—and Freud would prefer to have it that way—it is as if this theory had developed exclusively in the doctor's consulting-room and were unwelcome to everyone

[1] [First published simultaneously in the English and German editions of the same journal: translated by Cary F. Baynes, under the present title, in *Character and Personality: An International Quarterly of Psychodiagnostics and Allied Studies* (Durham, North Carolina), I:1 (Sept. 1932); and as "Sigmund Freud als kulturhistorische Erscheinung" (the original version) in *Charakter: eine Vierteljahresschrift für psychodiagnostische Studien und verwandte Gebiete* (Berlin), I:1 (Sept. 1932). Jung was a collaborating editor of the journal, along with Alfred Adler, Gordon W. Allport, Manfred Bleuler, Lucien Lévy-Bruhl, and others. The essay was reprinted in *Wirklichkeit der Seele* (Zurich, 1934).—EDITORS.]

but himself and a thorn in the flesh of "academic" science. And yet, even the most original and isolated idea does not drop down from heaven, but grows out of an objective network of thought which binds all contemporaries together whether they recognize it or not.

45   The historical conditions which preceded Freud were such that they made a phenomenon like himself necessary, and it is precisely the fundamental tenet of his teaching—namely, the repression of sexuality—that is most clearly conditioned in this historical sense. Like his greater contemporary Nietzsche, Freud stands at the end of the Victorian era, which was never given such an appropriate name on the Continent despite the fact that it was just as characteristic of the Germanic and Protestant countries as of the Anglo-Saxon. The Victorian era was an age of repression, of a convulsive attempt to keep anaemic ideals artificially alive in a framework of bourgeois respectability by constant moralizings. These ideals were the last offshoots of the collective religious ideas of the Middle Ages, and shortly before had been severely shaken by the French Enlightenment and the ensuing revolution. Hand in hand with this, ancient truths in the political field had become hollow and threatened to collapse. It was still too soon for the final overthrow, and consequently all through the nineteenth century frantic efforts were made to prevent the Christian Middle Ages from disappearing altogether. Political revolutions were stamped out, experiments in moral freedom were thwarted by middle-class public opinion, and the critical philosophy of the late eighteenth century reached its end in a renewed, systematic attempt to capture the world in a unified network of thought on the medieval model. But in the course of the nineteenth century enlightenment slowly broke through, particularly in the form of scientific materialism and rationalism.

46   This is the matrix out of which Freud grew, and its mental characteristics have shaped him along foreordained lines. He has a passion for explaining everything rationally, exactly as in the eighteenth century; one of his favourite maxims is Voltaire's "Écrasez l'infâme." With a certain satisfaction he invariably points out the flaw in the crystal; all complex psychic phenomena like art, philosophy, and religion fall under his suspicion and appear as "nothing but" repressions of the sexual instinct.

This essentially reductive and negative attitude of Freud's towards accepted cultural values is due to the historical conditions which immediately preceded him. He sees as his time forces him to see. This comes out most clearly in his book *The Future of an Illusion,* where he draws a picture of religion which corresponds exactly with the prejudices of a materialistic age.

47   Freud's revolutionary passion for negative explanations springs from the historical fact that the Victorian age falsified its cultural values in order to produce a middle-class view of the world, and, among the means employed, religion—or rather, the religion of repression—played the chief role. It is this sham religion that Freud has his eye on. The same is true of his idea of man: man's conscious qualities, his idealistically falsified persona, rest on a correspondingly dark background, that is to say on a basis of repressed infantile sexuality. Every positive gift or creative activity depends on some infantile negative quantity, in accordance with the materialistic *bon mot:* "Der Mensch ist, was er isst" (man is what he eats).

48   This conception of man, considered historically, is a reaction against the Victorian tendency to see everything in a rosy light and yet to describe everything *sub rosa.* It was an age of mental "pussyfooting" that finally gave birth to Nietzsche, who was driven to philosophize with a hammer. So it is only logical that ethical motives as determining factors in human life do not figure in Freud's teaching. He sees them in terms of conventional morality, which he justifiably supposes would not have existed in this form, or not have existed at all, if one or two bad-tempered patriarchs had not invented such precepts to protect themselves from the distressing consequences of their impotence. Since then these precepts have unfortunately gone on existing in the super-ego of every individual. This grotesquely depreciative view is a just punishment for the historical fact that the ethics of the Victorian age were nothing but conventional morality, the creation of curmudgeonly *praeceptores mundi.*

49   If Freud is viewed in this retrospective way as an exponent of the resentment of the new century against the old, with its illusions, its hypocrisy, its half-truths, its faked, overwrought emotions, its sickly morality, its bogus, sapless religiosity, and its lamentable taste, he can be seen, in my opinion, much more cor-

rectly than when one marks him out as the herald of new ways and new truths. He is a great destroyer who breaks the fetters of the past. He liberates us from the unwholesome pressure of a world of rotten habits. He shows how the values in which our parents believed may be understood in an altogether different sense: for instance, that sentimental fraud about the parents who live only for their children, or the noble son who worships his mother all his life, or the ideal daughter who completely understands her father. Previously these things were believed uncritically, but ever since Freud laid the unsavoury idea of incestuous fixation on the dining-room table as an object of discussion, salutary doubts have been aroused—though for reasons of health they should not be pushed too far.

50   The sexual theory, to be properly understood, should be taken as a negative critique of our contemporary psychology. We can become reconciled even to its most disturbing assertions if we know against what historical conditions they are directed. Once we know how the nineteenth century twisted perfectly natural facts into sentimental, moralistic virtues in order not to have its picture of the world upset, we can understand what Freud means by asserting that the infant already experiences sexuality at its mother's breast—an assertion which has aroused the greatest commotion. This interpretation casts suspicion on the proverbial innocence of the child at the breast, that is, on the mother-child relationship. That is the whole point of the assertion—it is a shot aimed at the heart of "holy motherhood." The fact that mothers bear children is not holy but merely natural. If people say it is holy, then one strongly suspects that something very unholy has to be covered up by it. Freud has said out loud "what is behind it," only he has unfortunately blackened the infant instead of the mother.

51   Scientifically, the theory of infantile sexuality is of little value. It is all one to the caterpillar whether we say that it eats its leaf with ordinary pleasure or with sexual pleasure. Freud's historical contribution does not consist in these scholastic mistakes of interpretation in the field of specialized science, but in the fact on which his fame is justifiably founded, namely that, like an Old Testament prophet, he overthrew false idols and pitilessly exposed to the light of day the rottenness of the contemporary psyche. Whenever he undertakes a painful reduction

(explaining the nineteenth-century God as a glorified version of Papa, or money-grubbing as infantile pleasure in excrement), we can be sure that a collective overvaluation or falsification is being attacked. Where, for instance, is the saccharine God of the nineteenth century confronted with a *deus absconditus,* as in Luther's teaching? And is it not assumed by all nice people that good men also earn good money?

52   Like Nietzsche, like the Great War, and like James Joyce, his literary counterpart, Freud is an answer to the sickness of the nineteenth century. That is indeed his chief significance. For those with a forward-looking view he offers no constructive plan, because not even with the boldest effort or the strongest will would it ever be possible to act out in real life all the repressed incest-wishes and other incompatibilities in the human psyche. On the contrary, Protestant ministers have already plunged into psychoanalysis because it seems to them an excellent means of sensitizing people's consciences to yet more sins than merely conscious ones—a truly grotesque but extremely logical turn of events prophesied years ago by Stanley Hall in his autobiography. Even the Freudians are beginning to take note of a new and if possible even more soulless repression—quite understandably, since no one knows what to do with his incompatible wishes. On the contrary, one begins to understand how unavoidable it is that such things are repressed.

53   In order to mitigate this cramp of conscience, Freud invented the idea of sublimation. Sublimation means nothing less than the alchemist's trick of turning the base into the noble, the bad into the good, the useless into the useful. Anyone who knew how to do this would be certain of immortal fame. Unfortunately, the secret of converting energy without the consumption of a still greater quantity of energy has never yet been discovered by the physicists. Sublimation remains, for the present, a pious wish-fulfilment invented for silencing inopportune questions.

54   In discussing these problems I do not wish to lay the main emphasis on the professional difficulties of the practising psychotherapist, but on the evident fact that Freud's programme is not a forward-looking one. Everything about it is oriented backwards. Freud's only interest is where things come from, never where they are going. It is more than the scientific need for caus-

ality that drives him to seek for causes, for otherwise it could not have escaped him that many psychological facts have explanations entirely different from those based on the *faux pas* of a *chronique scandaleuse*.

55   An excellent example of this is his essay on Leonardo da Vinci and the problem of the two mothers. As a matter of fact, Leonardo did have an illegitimate mother and a stepmother, but in reality the dual-mother problem may be present as a mythological motif even when the two mothers do not really exist. Mythical heroes very often have two mothers, and for the Pharaohs this mythological custom was actually *de rigueur*. But Freud stops short at the scurrilous fact; he contents himself with the idea that *naturally* something unpleasant or negative is concealed in the situation. Although this procedure is not exactly "scientific," yet, considered from the standpoint of historical justice, I credit it with a greater value than if it were scientifically unassailable. All too easily the dark background that is *also* present in the Leonardo problem could be rationalized away by a narrow scientific approach, and then Freud's historical task of showing up the darkness behind the false façades would not be fulfilled. A small scientific inaccuracy has little meaning here. If one goes through his works carefully and critically, one really does have the impression that Freud's aim of serving science, which he pushes again and again to the fore, has been secretly diverted to the cultural task of which he himself is unconscious, and that this has happened at the expense of the development of his theory. Today the voice of one crying in the wilderness must necessarily strike a scientific tone if the ear of the multitude is to be reached. At all costs we must be able to say that it is science which has brought such facts to light, for that alone is convincing. But even science is not proof against the unconscious *Weltanschauung*. How easy it would have been to take Leonardo's *St. Anne with the Virgin and the Christ Child* as a classical representation of the mythological motif of the two mothers! But for Freud's late Victorian psychology, and for an infinitely large public as well, it is far more effective if after "thorough investigation" it can be confirmed that the great artist owed his existence to a slip-up of his respectable father! This thrust goes home, and Freud makes this thrust not because he consciously wants to abandon science for gossip, but because he is under

compulsion from the *Zeitgeist* to expose the possible dark side of the human psyche. Yet the really scientific clue to the picture is the dual-mother motif, but that only stirs the few to whom knowledge really matters, however unfashionable it may be. Such an hypothesis leaves the greater public cold, because to them Freud's one-sided, negative explanation means very much more than it does to science.

56   It is axiomatic that science strives for an impartial, unbiased, and inclusive truth. The Freudian theory, on the other hand, is at best a partial truth, and therefore in order to maintain itself and be effective it has the rigidity of a dogma and the fanaticism of an inquisitor. For a scientific truth a simple statement suffices. Secretly, psychoanalytic theory has no intention of passing as a strict scientific truth; it aims rather at influencing a wider public. And from this we can recognize its origin in the doctor's consulting-room. It preaches those truths which it is of paramount importance that the neurotic of the early twentieth century should understand because he is an unconscious victim of late Victorian psychology. Psychoanalysis destroys the false values in him personally by cauterizing away the rottenness of the dead century. Thus far, it betokens a valuable, indeed indispensable increase in practical knowledge which has advanced the study of neurotic psychology in the most lasting way. We have to thank the bold one-sidedness of Freud if medicine is now in a position to treat cases of neurosis individually and make the individual psyche an object of research. Before Freud, this happened only as a rare curiosity.

57   But in so far as neurosis is not an illness specific to the Victorian era but enjoys a wide distribution in time and space, and is therefore found among people who are not in need of any special sexual enlightenment or the destruction of harmful assumptions in this respect, a theory of neurosis or of dreams which is based on a Victorian prejudice is at most of secondary importance to science. If this were not so, Adler's very different conception would have fallen flat and had no effect. Adler reduces everything not to the pleasure principle but to the power drive, and the success of his theory is not to be denied. This fact brings out with dazzling clearness the one-sidedness of the Freudian theory. Adler's, it is true, is just another one-sidedness, but taken together with Freud's it produces a more comprehensive and

still clearer picture of the resentment against the spirit of the nineteenth century. All the modern defection from the ideals of our fathers is mirrored again in Adler.

58   The human psyche, however, is not simply a product of the *Zeitgeist,* but is a thing of far greater constancy and immutability. The nineteenth century is a merely local and passing phenomenon, which has deposited but a thin layer of dust on the age-old psyche of mankind. Once this layer is wiped off and our professional eye-glasses are cleaned, what shall we see? How shall we look upon the psyche, and how shall we explain a neurosis? This problem confronts every analyst whose cases are not cured even after all the sexual experiences of childhood have been dug up, and all their cultural values dissected into lurid elements, or even when the patient has become that strange fiction—a "normal" man and a gregarious animal.

59   A general psychological theory that claims to be scientific should not be based on the malformations of the nineteenth century, and a theory of neurosis must also be capable of explaining hysteria among the Maori. As soon as the sexual theory leaves the narrow field of neurotic psychology and branches out into other fields, for instance that of primitive psychology, its one-sidedness and inadequacy leap to the eye. Insights that grew up from the observation of Viennese neuroses between 1890 and 1920 prove themselves poor tools when applied to the problems of totem and taboo, even when the application is made in a very skilful way. Freud has not penetrated into that deeper layer which is common to all men. He could not have done so without being untrue to his historical task. And this task he has fulfilled —a task enough for a whole life's work, and fully deserving the fame it has won.

IN MEMORY OF SIGMUND FREUD [1]

60   The cultural history of the past fifty years is inseparably bound up with the name of Sigmund Freud, the founder of psychoanalysis, who has just died. The Freudian outlook has affected practically every sphere of our contemporary thinking, except that of the exact sciences. Wherever the human psyche plays a decisive role, this outlook has left its mark, above all in the broad field of psychopathology, then in psychology, philosophy, aesthetics, ethnology and—last but not least—the psychology of religion. Everything that man can say about the nature of the psyche, whether it be true or only apparently true, necessarily touches upon the foundations of all the humane sciences, even though the really decisive discoveries have been made within the sphere of medicine, which, as we know, cannot be counted among the "humanities."

61   Freud was first and foremost a "nerve specialist" in the strictest sense of this word, and in every respect he always remained one. By training he was no psychiatrist, no psychologist, and no philosopher. In philosophy he lacked even the most rudimentary elements of education. He once assured me personally that it had never occurred to him to read Nietzsche. This fact is of importance in understanding Freud's peculiar views, which are distinguished by an apparently total lack of any philosophical premises. His theories bear the unmistakable stamp of the doctor's consulting-room. His constant point of departure is the neurotically degenerate psyche, unfolding its secrets with a mixture of reluctance and ill-concealed enjoyment under the critical eye of the doctor. But as the neurotic patient, besides having his individual sickness, is also an exponent of the local and

1 [Originally published as "Sigmund Freud: Ein Nachruf," *Sonntagsblatt der Basler Nachrichten*, XXXIII:40 (Oct. 1, 1939). Freud died in London on Sept. 23.—EDITORS.]

41

contemporary mentality, a bridge exists from the start between the doctor's view of his particular case and certain general assumptions. The existence of this bridge enabled Freud to turn his intuition from the narrow confines of the consulting-room to the wide world of moral, philosophical, and religious ideas, which also, unhappily enough, proved themselves amenable to this critical investigation.

62   Freud owed his initial impetus to Charcot, his great teacher at the Salpêtrière. The first fundamental lesson he learnt there was the teaching about hypnotism and suggestion, and in 1888 he translated Bernheim's book on the latter subject. The other was Charcot's discovery that hysterical symptoms were the consequence of certain ideas that had taken possession of the patient's "brain." Charcot's pupil, Pierre Janet, elaborated this theory in his comprehensive work *Névroses et idées fixes* and provided it with the necessary foundations. Freud's older colleague in Vienna, Joseph Breuer, furnished an illustrative case in support of this exceedingly important discovery (which, incidentally, had been made long before by many a family doctor), building upon it a theory of which Freud said that it "coincides with the medieval view once we substitute a psychological formula for the 'demon' of priestly fantasy." The medieval theory of possession (toned down by Janet to "obsession") was thus taken over by Breuer and Freud in a more positive form, the evil spirit—to reverse the Faustian miracle—being transmogrified into a harmless "psychological formula." It is greatly to the credit of both investigators that they did not, like the rationalistic Janet, gloss over the significant analogy with possession, but rather, following the medieval theory, hunted up the factor causing the possession in order, as it were, to exorcize the evil spirit. Breuer was the first to discover that the pathogenic "ideas" were memories of certain events which he called "traumatic." This discovery carried forward the preliminary work done at the Salpêtrière, and it laid the foundation of all Freud's theories. As early as 1893 both men recognized the far-reaching practical importance of their findings. They realized that the symptom-producing "ideas" were rooted in an *affect*. This affect had the peculiarity of never really coming to the surface, so that it was never really conscious. The task of the therapist was therefore to "abreact" the "blocked" affect.

63   This provisional formulation was certainly simple—too simple to do justice to the essence of the neuroses in general. At this point Freud commenced his own independent researches. It was first of all the question of the trauma that occupied him. He soon found (or thought he had found) that the traumatic factors were unconscious because of their painfulness. But they were painful because—according to his views at the time—they were one and all connected with the sphere of sex. The theory of the sexual trauma was Freud's first independent theory of hysteria. Every specialist who has to do with the neuroses knows on the one hand how suggestible the patients are and, on the other, how unreliable are their reports. The theory was therefore treading on slippery and treacherous ground. As a result, Freud soon felt compelled to correct it more or less tacitly by attributing the traumatic factor to an abnormal development of infantile fantasy. The motive force of this luxuriant fantasy-activity he took to be an infantile sexuality, which nobody had liked to speak of before. Cases of abnormal precocity of development had naturally long been known in the medical literature, but such had not been assumed to be the case in relatively normal children. Freud did not commit this mistake either, nor did he envisage any concrete form of precocious development. It was rather a question of his paraphrasing and interpreting more or less normal infantile occurrences in terms of sexuality. This view unleashed a storm of indignation and disgust, first of all in professional circles and then among the educated public. Apart from the fact that every radically new idea invariably provokes the most violent resistance of the experts, Freud's conception of the infant's instinctual life was an encroachment upon the domain of general and normal psychology, since his observations from the psychology of neurosis were transferred to a territory which had never before been exposed to this kind of illumination.

64   Careful and painstaking investigation of neurotic and, in particular, hysterical states of mind could not conceal from Freud that such patients often exhibit an unusually lively dream-life and on that account like to tell of their dreams. In structure and manner of expression their dreams frequently correspond to the symptomatology of their neurosis. Anxiety states and anxiety dreams go hand in hand and obviously spring from the same

43

root. Freud could therefore not avoid including dreams within the scope of his investigations. He had recognized very early that the "blocking" of the traumatic affect was due to the *repression* of "incompatible" material. The symptoms were substitutes for impulses, wishes, and fantasies which, because of their moral or aesthetic painfulness, were subjected to a "censorship" exercised by ethical conventions. In other words, they were pushed out of the conscious mind by a certain kind of moral attitude, and a specific inhibition prevented them from being remembered. The "theory of repression," as Freud aptly called it, became the centre-piece of his psychology. Since a great many things could be explained by this theory, it is not surprising that it was also applied to dreams. Freud's *Interpretation of Dreams* (1900) is an epoch-making work and probably the boldest attempt ever made to master the enigma of the unconscious psyche on the apparently firm ground of empiricism. Freud sought to prove with the aid of case material that dreams are disguised wish-fulfilments. This extension of the "repression mechanism," a concept borrowed from the psychology of neurosis, to the phenomenon of dreams was the second encroachment upon the sphere of normal psychology. It had immense consequences, as it stirred up problems which would have required for their solution a more compendious equipment than the limited experiences of the consulting-room.

65   *The Interpretation of Dreams* is probably Freud's most important work, and at the same time the most open to attack. For us young psychiatrists it was a fount of illumination, but for our older colleagues it was an object of mockery. As with his recognition that neurosis has the character of a medieval "possession," so, by treating dreams as a highly important source of information about the unconscious processes—"the dream is the *via regia* to the unconscious"—Freud rescued something of the utmost value from the past, where it had seemed irretrievably sunk in oblivion. Indeed, in ancient medicine as well as in the old religions, dreams had a lofty significance and the dignity of an oracle. At the turn of the century, however, it was an act of the greatest scientific courage to make anything as unpopular as dreams an object of serious discussion. What impressed us young psychiatrists most was neither the technique nor the theory, both of which seemed to us highly controversial, but the fact

that anyone should have dared to investigate dreams at all. This line of investigation opened the way to an understanding of schizophrenic hallucinations and delusions from the inside, whereas hitherto psychiatrists had been able to describe them only from the outside. More than that, *The Interpretation of Dreams* provided a key to the many locked doors in the psychology of neurotics as well as of normal people.

66   The repression theory was further applied to the interpretation of jokes, and in 1905 Freud published his entertaining *Jokes and Their Relation to the Unconscious,* a pendant to *The Psychopathology of Everyday Life.* Both these books may be read with enjoyment and instruction by the layman. A foray beyond the repression theory into the domain of primitive psychology, in *Totem and Taboo,* was less successful, since the application of concepts derived from the psychology of neurotics to the views of primitives did not explain the latter but only showed up the insufficiency of the former in a rather too obvious light.

67   The final application of this theory was to the field of religion, in *The Future of an Illusion* (1927). Though there is much that is still tenable in *Totem and Taboo,* the same cannot, unfortunately, be said of the latter work. Freud's inadequate training in philosophy and in the history of religion makes itself painfully conspicuous, quite apart from the fact that he had no understanding of what religion was about. In his old age he wrote a book on Moses, who led the children of Israel to the Promised Land but was not allowed to set foot in it himself. That his choice fell on Moses is probably no accident in the case of a personality like Freud.

68   As I said at the beginning, Freud always remained a physician. For all his interest in other fields, he constantly had the clinical picture of neurosis before his mind's eye—the very attitude that makes people ill and effectively prevents them from being healthy. Anyone who has this picture before him always sees the flaw in everything, and however much he may struggle against it, he must always point out what this daemonically obsessive picture compels him to see: the weak spot, the unadmitted wish, the hidden resentment, the secret, illegitimate fulfilment of a wish distorted by the "censor." The neurotic is ill precisely because such things haunt his psyche; for though his

unconscious contains many *other* things, it appears to be exclusively populated by contents that his consciousness has rejected for very good reasons. The keynote of Freud's thought is therefore a devastatingly pessimistic "nothing but." Nowhere does he break through to a vision of the helpful, healing powers which would let the unconscious be of some benefit to the patient. Every position is undermined by a psychological critique that reduces everything to its unfavourable or ambiguous elements, or at least makes one suspect that such elements exist. This negative attitude is undoubtedly correct when applied to the little games of make-believe which a neurosis produces in such abundance. Here the conjecture of unpleasant things in the background is often very much to the point, but not always. Also, there is no illness that is not at the same time an unsuccessful attempt at a cure. Instead of showing up the patient as the secret accomplice of morally inadmissible wishes, one can just as well explain him as the unwitting victim of instinctual problems which he doesn't understand and which nobody in his environment has helped him solve. His dreams, in particular, can be taken as nature's own auguries, having nothing whatever to do with the all-too-human self-deluding operations which Freud insinuates into the dream-process.

69   I say this not in order to criticize Freud's theories but to lay due emphasis on his scepticism towards all or most of the ideals of the nineteenth century. Freud has to be seen against this cultural background. He put his finger on more than one ulcerous spot. All that glittered in the nineteenth century was very far from being gold, religion included. Freud was a great destroyer, but the turn of the century offered so many opportunities for debunking that even Nietzsche was not enough. Freud completed the task, very thoroughly indeed. He aroused a wholesome mistrust in people and thereby sharpened their sense of real values. All that gush about man's innate goodness, which had addled so many brains after the dogma of original sin was no longer understood, was blown to the winds by Freud, and the little that remains will, let us hope, be driven out for good and all by the barbarism of the twentieth century. Freud was no prophet, but he is a prophetic figure. Like Nietzsche, he overthrew the gigantic idols of our day, and it remains to be seen whether our highest values are so real that their glitter is not

extinguished in the Acherontian flood. Doubt about our civilization and its values is the contemporary neurosis. If our convictions were really indubitable nobody would ever doubt them. Nor would anyone have been able to make it seem plausible that our ideals are only disguised expressions of motives that we do well to hide. But the nineteenth century has left us such a legacy of dubious propositions that doubt is not only possible but altogether justified, indeed meritorious. The gold will not prove its worth save in the fire. Freud has often been compared to a dentist, drilling out the carious tissue in the most painful manner. So far the comparison holds true, but not when it comes to the gold-filling. Freudian psychology does not fill the gap. If our critical reason tells us that in certain respects we are irrational and infantile, or that all religious beliefs are illusions, what are we to do about our irrationality, what are we to put in place of our exploded illusions? Our naïve childishness has in it the seeds of creativity, and illusion is a natural component of life, and neither of them can ever be suppressed or replaced by the rationalities and practicalities of convention.

70   Freud's psychology moves within the narrow confines of nineteenth-century scientific materialism. Its philosophical premises were never examined, thanks obviously to the Master's insufficient philosophical equipment. So it was inevitable that it should come under the influence of local and temporal prejudices—a fact that has been noted by various other critics. Freud's psychological method is and always was a cauterizing agent for diseased and degenerate material, such as is found chiefly in neurotic patients. It is an instrument to be used by a doctor, and it is dangerous and destructive, or at best ineffective, when applied to the natural expressions of life and its needs. A certain rigid one-sidedness in the theory, backed by an often fanatical intolerance, was perhaps an unavoidable necessity in the early decades of the century. Later, when the new ideas met with ample recognition, this grew into an aesthetic defect, and finally, like every fanaticism, it evoked the suspicion of an inner uncertainty. In the last resort, each of us carries the torch of knowledge only part of the way, and none is immune against error. Doubt alone is the mother of scientific truth. Whoever fights against dogma in high places falls victim, tragically enough, to the tyranny of a partial truth. All who had a share in

47

the fate of this great man saw this tragedy working out step by step in his life and increasingly narrowing his horizon.

71   In the course of the personal friendship which bound me to Freud for many years, I was permitted a deep glimpse into the mind of this remarkable man. He was a man possessed by a daemon—a man who had been vouchsafed an overwhelming revelation that took possession of his soul and never let him go. It was the encounter with Charcot's ideas that called awake in him that primordial image of a soul in the grip of a daemon, and kindled that passion for knowledge which was to lay open a dark continent to his gaze. He felt he had the key to the murky abysses of the possessed psyche. He wanted to unmask as illusion what the "absurd superstition" of the past took to be a devilish incubus, to whip away the disguises worn by the evil spirit and turn him back into a harmless poodle—in a word, reduce him to a "psychological formula." He believed in the power of the intellect; no Faustian shudderings tempered the hybris of his undertaking. He once said to me: "I only wonder what neurotics will do in the future when all their symbols have been unmasked. It will then be impossible to have a neurosis." He expected enlightenment to do everything—his favourite quotation was Voltaire's "Écrasez l'infâme." From this sentiment there grew up his astonishing knowledge and understanding of any morbid psychic material, which he smelt out under a hundred disguises and was able to bring to light with truly unending patience.

72   Ludwig Klages' saying that "the spirit is the adversary of the soul" [2] might serve as a cautionary motto for the way Freud approached the possessed psyche. Whenever he could, he dethroned the "spirit" as the possessing and repressing agent by reducing it to a "psychological formula." Spirit, for him, was just a "nothing but." In a crucial talk with him I once tried to get him to understand the admonition: "Try the spirits whether they are of God" (I John 4 : 1). In vain. Thus fate had to take its course. For one can fall victim to possession if one does not understand betimes why one is possessed. One should ask oneself for once: Why has this idea taken possession of me? What does that mean in regard to myself? A modest doubt like this can save

2 [Cf. Klages, *Der Geist als Widersacher der Seele;* and Jung, *Civilization in Transition,* pars. 375, 657.—EDITORS.]

us from falling head first into the idea and vanishing for ever.

73   Freud's "psychological formula" is only an apparent substitute for the daemonically vital thing that causes a neurosis. In reality only the spirit can cast out the "spirits"—not the intellect, which at best is a mere assistant, like Faust's Wagner, and scarcely fitted to play the role of an exorcist.

III

RICHARD WILHELM: IN MEMORIAM

RICHARD WILHELM: IN MEMORIAM [1]

74   It is no easy task for me to speak of Richard Wilhelm and his work, because, starting very far away from one another, our paths crossed in cometlike fashion. His life-work has a range that lies outside my compass. I have never seen the China that first moulded his thought and later continued to engross him, nor am I familiar with its language, the living expression of the Chinese East. I stand indeed as a stranger outside that vast realm of knowledge and experience in which Wilhelm worked as a master of his profession. He as a sinologist and I as a doctor would probably never have come into contact had we remained specialists. But we met in a field of humanity which begins beyond the academic boundary posts. There lay our point of contact; there the spark leapt across and kindled a light that was to become for me one of the most significant events of my life. Because of this I may perhaps speak of Wilhelm and his work, thinking with grateful respect of this mind which created a bridge between East and West and gave to the Occident the precious heritage of a culture thousands of years old, a culture perhaps destined to disappear forever.

75   Wilhelm possessed the kind of mastery which is won only by a man who goes beyond his speciality, and so his striving for

---

1 [Originally delivered as the principal address at a memorial service held in Munich in May, 1930, for Wilhelm, who had died the previous March 1. Published as "Nachruf für Richard Wilhelm," *Neue Zürcher Zeitung*, CLI:1 (March 6, 1930), and in the *Chinesisch-Deutscher Almanach* (Frankfurt a. M.), 1931. Republished in the 2nd edition of Jung and Wilhelm, *Das Geheimnis der goldenen Blüte: Ein chinesisches Lebensbuch* (Zurich, 1938). Previously translated by Cary F. Baynes as an appendix to Jung and Wilhelm, *The Secret of the Golden Flower* (London and New York, 1931; revised and augmented edition, 1962). Grateful acknowledgment is made here to Mrs. Baynes for permission to draw upon the 1962 version of her translation. For Jung's commentary on *The Secret of the Golden Flower*, see *Coll. Works*, Vol. 13.—EDITORS.]

knowledge became a concern touching all mankind. Or rather, it had been that from the beginning and remained so always. What else could have liberated him so completely from the narrow horizon of the European—and indeed, of the missionary— that no sooner had he delved into the secrets of the Chinese mind than he perceived the treasure hidden there for us, and sacrificed his European prejudices for the sake of this rare pearl? Only an all-embracing humanity, a greatness of heart that glimpses the whole, could have enabled him to open himself without reserve to a profoundly alien spirit, and to further its influence by putting his manifold gifts and capacities at its service. The understanding with which he devoted himself to this task, with no trace of Christian resentment or European arrogance, bears witness to a truly great mind; for all mediocre minds in contact with a foreign culture either perish in the blind attempt to deracinate themselves or else they indulge in an uncomprehending and presumptuous passion for criticism. Toying only with the surface and externals of the foreign culture, they never eat its bread or drink its wine, and so never enter into a real communion of minds, that most intimate transfusion and interpenetration which generates a new birth.

76   As a rule, the specialist's is a purely masculine mind, an intellect to which fecundity is an alien and unnatural process; it is therefore an especially ill-adapted tool for giving rebirth to a foreign spirit. But a larger mind bears the stamp of the feminine; it is endowed with a receptive and fruitful womb which can reshape what is strange and give it a familiar form. Wilhelm possessed the rare gift of a maternal intellect. To it he owed his unequalled ability to feel his way into the spirit of the East and to make his incomparable translations.

77   To me the greatest of his achievements is his translation of, and commentary on, the *I Ching*.[2] Before I came to know Wilhelm's translation, I had worked for years with Legge's inadequate rendering,[3] and I was therefore fully able to appreciate the extraordinary difference between the two. Wilhelm has succeeded in bringing to life again, in new form, this ancient work

2 [Wilhelm's translation of the Chinese classic was published in Jena, 1924. Translated into English by Cary F. Baynes as *The I Ching, or Book of Changes* (1950), with a foreword by Jung (see *Coll. Works*, Vol. 11).—EDITORS.]

3 *The Yi King*, trans. by James Legge (Sacred Books of the East, Vol. 16; 1882).

in which not only many sinologists but most of the modern Chinese see nothing more than a collection of absurd magical spells. This book embodies, as perhaps no other, the living spirit of Chinese civilization, for the best minds of China have collaborated on it and contributed to it for thousands of years. Despite its fabulous age it has never grown old, but still lives and works, at least for those who seek to understand its meaning. That we too belong to this favoured group we owe to the creative achievement of Wilhelm. He has brought the book closer to us by his careful translation and personal experience both as a pupil of a Chinese master of the old school and as an initiate in the psychology of Chinese yoga, who made constant use of the *I Ching* in practice.

78   But together with these rich gifts, Wilhelm has bequeathed to us a task whose magnitude we can only surmise at present, but cannot fully apprehend. Anyone who, like myself, has had the rare good fortune to experience in association with Wilhelm the divinatory power of the *I Ching* cannot remain ignorant of the fact that we have here an Archimedean point from which our Western attitude of mind could be lifted off its foundations. It is no small service to have given us, as Wilhelm did, such a comprehensive and richly coloured picture of a foreign culture. What is even more important is that he has inoculated us with the living germ of the Chinese spirit, capable of working a fundamental change in our view of the world. We are no longer reduced to being admiring or critical observers, but find ourselves partaking of the spirit of the East to the extent that we succeed in experiencing the living power of the *I Ching*.

79   The principle on which the use of the *I Ching* is based appears at first sight to be in complete contradiction to our scientific and causal thinking. For us it is unscientific in the extreme, almost taboo, and therefore outside the scope of our scientific judgment, indeed incomprehensible to it.

80   Some years ago, the then president of the British Anthropological Society asked me how it was that so highly intelligent a people as the Chinese had produced no science. I replied that this must be an optical illusion, since the Chinese did have a science whose standard text-book was the *I Ching*, but that the principle of this science, like so much else in China, was altogether different from the principle of our science.

81   The science of the *I Ching* is based not on the causality principle but on one which—hitherto unnamed because not familiar to us—I have tentatively called the *synchronistic* principle. My researches into the psychology of unconscious processes long ago compelled me to look around for another principle of explanation, since the causality principle seemed to me insufficient to explain certain remarkable manifestations of the unconscious. I found that there are psychic parallelisms which simply cannot be related to each other causally, but must be connected by another kind of principle altogether. This connection seemed to lie essentially in the relative simultaneity of the events, hence the term "synchronistic." It seems as though time, far from being an abstraction, is a concrete continuum which possesses qualities or basic conditions capable of manifesting themselves simultaneously in different places by means of an acausal parallelism, such as we find, for instance, in the simultaneous occurrence of identical thoughts, symbols, or psychic states. Another example, pointed out by Wilhelm, would be the coincidence of Chinese and European periods of style, which cannot have been causally related to one another. Astrology would be an example of synchronicity on a grand scale if only there were enough thoroughly tested findings to support it. But at least we have at our disposal a number of well-tested and statistically verifiable facts which make the problem of astrology seem worthy of scientific investigation. Its value is obvious enough to the psychologist, since astrology represents the sum of all the psychological knowledge of antiquity.

82   The fact that it is possible to reconstruct a person's character fairly accurately from his birth data shows the relative validity of astrology. It must be remembered, however, that the birth data are in no way dependent on the actual astronomical constellations, but are based on an arbitrary, purely conceptual time system. Owing to the precession of the equinoxes, the spring-point has long since moved out of the constellation of Aries into Pisces, so that the astrological zodiac on which horoscopes are calculated no longer corresponds to the heavenly one. If there are any astrological diagnoses of character that are in fact correct, this is due not to the influence of the stars but to our own hypothetical time qualities. In other words, whatever is

born or done at this particular moment of time has the quality of this moment of time.

83   Here we have the basic formula for the use of the *I Ching*. As you know, the hexagram that characterizes the moment of time, and gives us insight into it, is obtained by manipulating a bundle of yarrow stalks or by throwing three coins. The division of the yarrow stalks or the fall of the coins depends on pure chance. The runic stalks or coins fall into the pattern of the moment. The only question is: Did King Wen and the Duke of Chou, who lived a thousand years before the birth of Christ, interpret these chance patterns correctly? [4] Experience alone can decide.

84   At his first lecture at the Psychological Club in Zurich, Wilhelm, at my request, demonstrated the use of the *I Ching* and at the same time made a prognosis which, in less than two years, was fulfilled to the letter and with the utmost clarity. Predictions of this kind could be further confirmed by numerous parallel experiences. However, I am not concerned with establishing objectively the validity of the *I Ching*'s statements, but take it simply as a premise, just as Wilhelm did. I am concerned only with the astonishing fact that the hidden qualities of the moment become legible in the hexagram. The interconnection of events made evident by the *I Ching* is essentially analogous to what we find in astrology. There the moment of birth corresponds to the fall of the coins, the constellation to the hexagram, and the astrological interpretation of the birth data corresponds to the text assigned to the hexagram.

85   The type of thinking based on the synchronistic principle, which reached its climax in the *I Ching*, is the purest expression of Chinese thinking in general. In the West it has been absent from the history of philosophy since the time of Heraclitus, and reappears only as a faint echo in Leibniz.[5] However, in the interim it was not altogether extinguished, but lingered on in the twilight of astrological speculation, and it still remains on that level today.

86   At this point the *I Ching* responds to something in us that is

[4] For the details and history of the method, see the *I Ching* (1967 edn.), pp. xlixff. and 356ff.

[5] [See Hellmut Wilhelm, "The Concept of Time in the Book of Changes," pp. 216ff.—EDITORS.]

in need of further development. Occultism has enjoyed a renaissance in our times that is without parallel—the light of the Western mind is nearly darkened by it. I am not thinking now of our seats of learning and their representatives. As a doctor who deals with ordinary people, I know that the universities have ceased to act as disseminators of light. People are weary of scientific specialization and rationalism and intellectualism. They want to hear truths that broaden rather than restrict, that do not obscure but enlighten, that do not run off them like water but penetrate them to the marrow. This search is only too likely to lead a large if anonymous public astray.

87   When I think of the significance of Wilhelm's achievement, I am always reminded of Anquetil Duperron, the Frenchman who brought the first translation of the Upanishads to Europe. This was at the very time when, after almost eighteen hundred years, the inconceivable happened and the Goddess of Reason drove the Christian God from his throne in Notre-Dame. Today, when far more inconceivable things are happening in Russia than ever did in Paris, and Christianity has become so debilitated that even the Buddhists think it is high time they sent missionaries to Europe, it is Wilhelm who brings new light from the East. This was the cultural task to which he felt himself called, recognizing how much the East had to offer in our spiritual need.

88   A beggar is not helped by having alms, great or small, pressed into his hand, even though this may be what he wants. He is far better helped if we show him how he can permanently rid himself of his beggary by work. Unfortunately, the spiritual beggars of our time are too inclined to accept the alms of the East in bulk and to imitate its ways unthinkingly. This is a danger about which too many warnings cannot be uttered, and one which Wilhelm felt very clearly. The spirit of Europe is not helped merely by new sensations or a titillation of the nerves. What it has taken China thousands of years to build cannot be acquired by theft. If we want to possess it, we must earn the right to it by working on ourselves. Of what use to us is the wisdom of the Upanishads or the insight of Chinese yoga if we desert our own foundations as though they were errors outlived, and, like homeless pirates, settle with thievish intent on foreign shores? The insights of the East, and in particular the wisdom of

the *I Ching*, have no meaning for us if we close our minds to our own problems, jog along with our conventional prejudices, and veil from ourselves our real human nature with all its dangerous undercurrents and darknesses. The light of this wisdom shines only in the dark, not in the brightly lit theatre of our European consciousness and will. The wisdom of the *I Ching* issued from a background of whose horrors we have a faint inkling when we read of Chinese massacres, of the sinister power of Chinese secret societies, or of the nameless poverty, hopeless filth and vices of the Chinese masses.

89   We need to have a firmly based, three-dimensional life of our own before we can experience the wisdom of the East as a living thing. Therefore, our prime need is to learn a few European truths about ourselves. Our way begins with European reality and not with yoga exercises which would only delude us about our own reality. We must continue Wilhelm's work of translation in a wider sense if we wish to show ourselves worthy pupils of the master. The central concept of Chinese philosophy is *tao*, which Wilhelm translated as "meaning." Just as Wilhelm gave the spiritual treasure of the East a European meaning, so we should translate this meaning into life. To do this—that is, to realize *tao*—would be the true task of the pupil.

90   If we turn our eyes to the East, we see an overwhelming destiny fulfilling itself. The guns of Europe have burst open the gates of Asia; European science and technology, European materialism and cupidity, are flooding China. We have conquered the East politically. And what happened when Rome did the same thing to the Near East? The spirit of the East entered Rome. Mithras, the Persian god of light, became the god of the Roman legions, and out of the most unlikely corner of Asia Minor a new spiritual Rome arose. Would it be unthinkable that the same thing might happen today and find us just as blind as the cultured Romans who marvelled at the superstitions of the Christians? It is worth noticing that England and Holland, the two main colonizing powers in Asia, are also the two most infected with Hindu theosophy. I know that our unconscious is full of Eastern symbolism. The spirit of the East is really at our gates. Therefore it seems to me that the search for *tao*, for a meaning in life, has already become a collective phenomenon among us, and to a far greater extent than is generally realized.

The fact that Wilhelm and the indologist Hauer were asked to lecture on yoga at this year's congress of German psychotherapists is a most significant sign of the times. Imagine what it means when a practising physician, who has to deal with people at their most sensitive and receptive, establishes contact with an Eastern system of healing! In this way the spirit of the East penetrates through all our pores and reaches the most vulnerable places of Europe. It could be a dangerous infection, but it might also be a remedy. The Babylonian confusion of tongues in the West has created such a disorientation that everyone longs for simpler truths, or at least for guiding ideas which speak not to the head alone but also to the heart, which bring clarity to the contemplative spirit and peace to the restless pressure of our feelings. Like ancient Rome, we today are once more importing every form of exotic superstition in the hope of finding the right remedy for our sickness.

91 Human instinct knows that all great truth is simple. The man whose instincts are atrophied therefore supposes that it is found in cheap simplifications and platitudes; or, as a result of his disappointment, he falls into the opposite error of thinking that it must be as obscure and complicated as possible. Today we have a Gnostic movement in the anonymous masses which is the exact psychological counterpart of the Gnostic movement nineteen hundred years ago. Then, as today, solitary wanderers like Apollonius of Tyana spun the spiritual threads from Europe to Asia, perhaps to remotest India. Viewing him in this historical perspective, I see Wilhelm as one of those great Gnostic intermediaries who brought the Hellenic spirit into contact with the cultural heritage of the East and thereby caused a new world to rise out of the ruins of the Roman Empire.

92 In the midst of the jarring disharmony of European opinion and the shouts of false prophets, it is indeed a blessing to hear the simple language of Wilhelm, the messenger from China. One notices at once that it is schooled in the plant-like spontaneity of the Chinese mind, which is able to express profound things in simple language. It discloses something of the simplicity of great truth, the ingenuousness of deep meaning, and it carries to us the delicate perfume of the Golden Flower. Penetrating gently, it has set in the soil of Europe a tender seedling,

giving us a new intuition of life and its meaning, far removed from the tension and arrogance of the European will.

93   Faced with the alien culture of the East, Wilhelm showed a degree of modesty highly unusual in a European. He approached it freely, without prejudice, without the assumption of knowing better; he opened his heart and mind to it. He let himself be gripped and shaped by it, so that when he came back to Europe he brought us, not only in his spirit but in his whole being, a true image of the East. This deep transformation was certainly not won without great sacrifice, for our historical premises are so entirely different. The keenness of Western consciousness and its harsh problems had to soften before the more universal, more equable nature of the East; Western rationalism and one-sided differentiation had to yield to Eastern breadth and simplicity. For Wilhelm this change meant not only a shifting of the intellectual standpoint but a radical rearrangement of the components of his personality. The picture of the East he has given us, free of ulterior motive and all trace of tendentiousness, could never have been painted in such perfection had he not been able to let the European in him slip into the background. If he had allowed East and West to clash together with unyielding harshness, he could not have fulfilled his mission of conveying to us a true picture of China. The sacrifice of the European was unavoidable and necessary for the fulfilment of the task fate laid upon him.

94   Wilhelm accomplished his mission in every sense of the word. Not only did he make accessible to us the cultural treasure of ancient China, but, as I have said, he brought us its spiritual root, the root that has remained alive all these thousands of years, and planted it in the soil of Europe. With the completion of this task, his mission reached its climax and, unfortunately, its end. According to the law of *enantiodromia,* so well understood by the Chinese, the end of one phase is the beginning of its opposite. Thus *yang* at its highest point changes into *yin,* and positive into negative. I came closer to Wilhelm only in the last years of his life, and I could observe how, with the completion of his life-work, Europe and European man hemmed him in more and more closely, beset him in fact. And at the same time there grew in him the feeling that he stood on the brink of a great

change, an upheaval whose nature he could not clearly grasp. He only knew that he faced a decisive crisis. His physical illness went parallel with this development. His dreams were filled with memories of China, but the images were always sad and gloomy, a clear proof that the Chinese contents of his mind had become negative.

95   Nothing can be sacrificed for ever. Everything returns later in changed form, and when once a great sacrifice has been made, the sacrificed thing when it returns must meet with a healthy and resistant body that can take the shock. Therefore, a spiritual crisis of these dimensions often means death if it takes place in a body weakened by disease. For now the sacrificial knife is in the hand of him who was sacrificed, and a death is demanded of the erstwhile sacrificer.

96   As you see, I have not withheld my personal views, for if I had not told you what Wilhelm meant to me, how would it have been possible for me to speak of him? Wilhelm's life-work is of such immense importance to me because it clarified and confirmed so much that I had been seeking, striving for, thinking, and doing in my efforts to alleviate the psychic sufferings of Europeans. It was a tremendous experience for me to hear through him, in clear language, things I had dimly divined in the confusion of our European unconscious. Indeed, I feel myself so very much enriched by him that it seems to me as if I had received more from him than from any other man. That is also the reason why I do not feel it a presumption if I am the one to offer on the altar of his memory the gratitude and respect of all of us.

IV

ON THE RELATION OF
ANALYTICAL PSYCHOLOGY TO POETRY

PSYCHOLOGY AND LITERATURE

ON THE RELATION OF ANALYTICAL
PSYCHOLOGY TO POETRY [1]

97   In spite of its difficulty, the task of discussing the relation of
analytical psychology to poetry affords me a welcome opportunity to define my views on the much debated question of the
relations between psychology and art in general. Although the
two things cannot be compared, the close connections which undoubtedly exist between them call for investigation. These
connections arise from the fact that the practice of art is a psychological activity and, as such, can be approached from a
psychological angle. Considered in this light, art, like any other
human activity deriving from psychic motives, is a proper subject for psychology. This statement, however, involves a very
definite limitation of the psychological viewpoint when we come
to apply it in practice. Only that aspect of art which consists in
the process of artistic creation can be a subject for psychological
study, but not that which constitutes its essential nature. The
question of what art is in itself can never be answered by the
psychologist, but must be approached from the side of aesthetics.

98   A similar distinction must be made in the realm of religion.
A psychological approach is permissible only in regard to the
emotions and symbols which constitute the phenomenology of
religion, but which do not touch upon its essential nature. If the
essence of religion and art could be explained, then both of
them would become mere subdivisions of psychology. This is

[1] [A lecture delivered to the Society for German Language and Literature,
Zurich, May, 1922. First published as "Über die Beziehungen der analytischen
Psychologie zum dichterischen Kunstwerk," *Wissen und Leben* (Zurich), XV:19-
20 (Sept., 1922); reprinted in *Seelenprobleme der Gegenwart* (Zurich, 1931);
translated by H. G. Baynes, as "On the Relation of Analytical Psychology to
Poetic Art," *British Journal of Psychology* (Medical Section) (Cambridge), III:3
(1923), reprinted in *Contributions to Analytical Psychology* (London and New
York, 1928).—EDITORS.]

not to say that such violations of their nature have not been attempted. But those who are guilty of them obviously forget that a similar fate might easily befall psychology, since its intrinsic value and specific quality would be destroyed if it were regarded as a mere activity of the brain, and were relegated along with the endocrine functions to a subdivision of physiology. This too, as we know, has been attempted.

99   Art by its very nature is not science, and science by its very nature is not art; both these spheres of the mind have something in reserve that is peculiar to them and can be explained only in its own terms. Hence when we speak of the relation of psychology to art, we shall treat only of that aspect of art which can be submitted to psychological scrutiny without violating its nature. Whatever the psychologist has to say about art will be confined to the process of artistic creation and has nothing to do with its innermost essence. He can no more explain this than the intellect can describe or even understand the nature of feeling. Indeed, art and science would not exist as separate entities at all if the fundamental difference between them had not long since forced itself on the mind. The fact that artistic, scientific, and religious propensities still slumber peacefully together in the small child, or that with primitives the beginnings of art, science, and religion coalesce in the undifferentiated chaos of the magical mentality, or that no trace of "mind" can be found in the natural instincts of animals—all this does nothing to prove the existence of a unifying principle which alone would justify a reduction of the one to the other. For if we go so far back into the history of the mind that the distinctions between its various fields of activity become altogether invisible, we do not reach an underlying principle of their unity, but merely an earlier, undifferentiated state in which no separate activities yet exist. But the elementary state is not an explanatory principle that would allow us to draw conclusions as to the nature of later, more highly developed states, even though they must necessarily derive from it. A scientific attitude will always tend to overlook the peculiar nature of these more differentiated states in favour of their causal derivation, and will endeavour to subordinate them to a general but more elementary principle.

100   These theoretical reflections seem to me very much in place today, when we so often find that works of art, and particularly

poetry, are interpreted precisely in this manner, by reducing them to more elementary states. Though the material he works with and its individual treatment can easily be traced back to the poet's personal relations with his parents, this does not enable us to understand his poetry. The same reduction can be made in all sorts of other fields, and not least in the case of pathological disturbances. Neuroses and psychoses are likewise reducible to infantile relations with the parents, and so are a man's good and bad habits, his beliefs, peculiarities, passions, interests, and so forth. It can hardly be supposed that all these very different things must have exactly the same explanation, for otherwise we would be driven to the conclusion that they actually are the same thing. If a work of art is explained in the same way as a neurosis, then either the work of art is a neurosis or a neurosis is a work of art. This explanation is all very well as a play on words, but sound common sense rebels against putting a work of art on the same level as a neurosis. An analyst might, in an extreme case, view a neurosis as a work of art through the lens of his professional bias, but it would never occur to an intelligent layman to mistake a pathological phenomenon for art, in spite of the undeniable fact that a work of art arises from much the same psychological conditions as a neurosis. This is only natural, because certain of these conditions are present in every individual and, owing to the relative constancy of the human environment, are constantly the same, whether in the case of a nervous intellectual, a poet, or a normal human being. All have had parents, all have a father- or a mother-complex, all know about sex and therefore have certain common and typical human difficulties. One poet may be influenced more by his relation to his father, another by the tie to his mother, while a third shows unmistakable traces of sexual repression in his poetry. Since all this can be said equally well not only of every neurotic but of every normal human being, nothing specific is gained for the judgment of a work of art. At most our knowledge of its psychological antecedents will have been broadened and deepened.

101   The school of medical psychology inaugurated by Freud has undoubtedly encouraged the literary historian to bring certain peculiarities of a work of art into relation with the intimate, personal life of the poet. But this is nothing new in principle,

for it has long been known that the scientific treatment of art will reveal the personal threads that the artist, intentionally or unintentionally, has woven into his work. The Freudian approach may, however, make possible a more exhaustive demonstration of the influences that reach back into earliest childhood and play their part in artistic creation. To this extent the psychoanalysis of art differs in no essential from the subtle psychological nuances of a penetrating literary analysis. The difference is at most a question of degree, though we may occasionally be surprised by indiscreet references to things which a rather more delicate touch might have passed over if only for reasons of tact. This lack of delicacy seems to be a professional peculiarity of the medical psychologist, and the temptation to draw daring conclusions easily leads to flagrant abuses. A slight whiff of scandal often leads spice to a biography, but a little more becomes a nasty inquisitiveness—bad taste masquerading as science. Our interest is insidiously deflected from the work of art and gets lost in the labyrinth of psychic determinants, the poet becomes a clinical case and, very likely, yet another addition to the curiosa of *psychopathia sexualis*. But this means that the psychoanalysis of art has turned aside from its proper objective and strayed into a province that is as broad as mankind, that is not in the least specific of the artist and has even less relevance to his art.

102   This kind of analysis brings the work of art into the sphere of general human psychology, where many other things besides art have their origin. To explain art in these terms is just as great a platitude as the statement that "every artist is a narcissist." Every man who pursues his own goal is a "narcissist"—though one wonders how permissible it is to give such wide currency to a term specifically coined for the pathology of neurosis. The statement therefore amounts to nothing; it merely elicits the faint surprise of a *bon mot*. Since this kind of analysis is in no way concerned with the work of art itself, but strives like a mole to bury itself in the dirt as speedily as possible, it always ends up in the common earth that unites all mankind. Hence its explanations have the same tedious monotony as the recitals which one daily hears in the consulting-room.

103   The reductive method of Freud is a purely medical one, and the treatment is directed at a pathological or otherwise unsuitable formation which has taken the place of the normal func-

tioning. It must therefore be broken down, and the way cleared for healthy adaptation. In this case, reduction to the common human foundation is altogether appropriate. But when applied to a work of art it leads to the results I have described. It strips the work of art of its shimmering robes and exposes the nakedness and drabness of *Homo sapiens,* to which species the poet and artist also belong. The golden gleam of artistic creation—the original object of discussion—is extinguished as soon as we apply to it the same corrosive method which we use in analysing the fantasies of hysteria. The results are no doubt very interesting and may perhaps have the same kind of scientific value as, for instance, a post-mortem examination of the brain of Nietzsche, which might conceivably show us the particular atypical form of paralysis from which he died. But what would this have to do with *Zarathustra?* Whatever its subterranean background may have been, is it not a whole world in itself, beyond the human, all-too-human imperfections, beyond the world of migraine and cerebral atrophy?

104   I have spoken of Freud's reductive method but have not stated in what that method consists. It is essentially a medical technique for investigating morbid psychic phenomena, and it is solely concerned with the ways and means of getting round or peering through the foreground of consciousness in order to reach the psychic background, or the unconscious. It is based on the assumption that the neurotic patient represses certain psychic contents because they are morally incompatible with his conscious values. It follows that the repressed contents must have correspondingly negative traits—infantile-sexual, obscene, or even criminal—which make them unacceptable to consciousness. Since no man is perfect, everyone must possess such a background whether he admits it or not. Hence it can always be exposed if only one uses the technique of interpretation worked out by Freud.

105   In the short space of a lecture I cannot, of course, enter into the details of the technique. A few hints must suffice. The unconscious background does not remain inactive, but betrays itself by its characteristic effects on the contents of consciousness. For example, it produces fantasies of a peculiar nature, which can easily be interpreted as sexual images. Or it produces characteristic disturbances of the conscious processes, which again

can be reduced to repressed contents. A very important source for knowledge of the unconscious contents is provided by dreams, since these are direct products of the activity of the unconscious. The essential thing in Freud's reductive method is to collect all the clues pointing to the unconscious background, and then, through the analysis and interpretation of this material, to reconstruct the elementary instinctual processes. Those conscious contents which give us a clue to the unconscious background are incorrectly called *symbols* by Freud. They are not true symbols, however, since according to his theory they have merely the role of *signs* or *symptoms* of the subliminal processes. The true symbol differs essentially from this, and should be understood as an expression of an intuitive idea that cannot yet be formulated in any other or better way. When Plato, for instance, puts the whole problem of the theory of knowledge in his parable of the cave, or when Christ expresses the idea of the Kingdom of Heaven in parables, these are genuine and true symbols, that is, attempts to express something for which no verbal concept yet exists. If we were to interpret Plato's metaphor in Freudian terms we would naturally arrive at the uterus, and would have proved that even a mind like Plato's was still struck on a primitive level of infantile sexuality. But we would have completely overlooked what Plato actually created out of the primitive determinants of his philosophical ideas; we would have missed the essential point and merely discovered that he had infantile-sexual fantasies like any other mortal. Such a discovery could be of value only for a man who regarded Plato as superhuman, and who can now state with satisfaction that Plato too was an ordinary human being. But who would want to regard Plato as a god? Surely only one who is dominated by infantile fantasies and therefore possesses a neurotic mentality. For him the reduction to common human truths is salutary on medical grounds, but this would have nothing whatever to do with the meaning of Plato's parable.

106   I have purposely dwelt on the application of medical psychoanalysis to works of art because I want to emphasize that the psychoanalytic method is at the same time an essential part of the Freudian doctrine. Freud himself by his rigid dogmatism has ensured that the method and the doctrine—in themselves two very different things—are regarded by the public as identical.

Yet the method may be employed with beneficial results in medical cases without at the same time exalting it into a doctrine.
And against this doctrine we are bound to raise vigorous objec-
tions. The assumptions it rests on are quite arbitrary. For
example, neuroses are by no means exclusively caused by sexual
repression, and the same holds true for psychoses. There is no
foundation for saying that dreams merely contain repressed
wishes whose moral incompatibility requires them to be disguised by a hypothetical dream-censor. The Freudian technique
of interpretation, so far as it remains under the influence of its
own one-sided and therefore erroneous hypotheses, displays a
quite obvious bias.

107   In order to do justice to a work of art, analytical psychology
must rid itself entirely of medical prejudice; for a work of art is
not a disease, and consequently requires a different approach
from the medical one. A doctor naturally has to seek out the
causes of a disease in order to pull it up by the roots, but just as
naturally the psychologist must adopt exactly the opposite attitude towards a work of art. Instead of investigating its typically
human determinants, he will inquire first of all into its meaning, and will concern himself with its determinants only in so far
as they enable him to understand it more fully. Personal causes
have as much or as little to do with a work of art as the soil with
the plant that springs from it. We can certainly learn to understand some of the plant's peculiarities by getting to know its
habitat, and for the botanist this is an important part of his
equipment. But nobody will maintain that everything essential
has then been discovered about the plant itself. The personal
orientation which the doctor needs when confronted with the
question of aetiology in medicine is quite out of place in dealing
with a work of art, just because a work of art is not a human
being, but is something supra-personal. It is a thing and not a
personality; hence it cannot be judged by personal criteria. Indeed, the special significance of a true work of art resides in the
fact that it has escaped from the limitations of the personal and
has soared beyond the personal concerns of its creator.

108   I must confess from my own experience that it is not at all
easy for a doctor to lay aside his professional bias when considering a work of art and look at it with a mind cleared of the current biological causality. But I have come to learn that although

a psychology with a purely biological orientation can explain a good deal about man in general, it cannot be applied to a work of art and still less to man as creator. A purely causalistic psychology is only able to reduce every human individual to a member of the species *Homo sapiens,* since its range is limited to what is transmitted by heredity or derived from other sources. But a work of art is not transmitted or derived—it is a creative reorganization of those very conditions to which a causalistic psychology must always reduce it. The plant is not a mere product of the soil; it is a living, self-contained process which in essence has nothing to do with the character of the soil. In the same way, the meaning and individual quality of a work of art inhere within it and not in its extrinsic determinants. One might almost describe it as a living being that uses man only as a nutrient medium, employing his capacities according to its own laws and shaping itself to the fulfilment of its own creative purpose.

109   But here I am anticipating somewhat, for I have in mind a particular type of art which I still have to introduce. Not every work of art originates in the way I have just described. There are literary works, prose as well as poetry, that spring wholly from the author's intention to produce a particular result. He submits his material to a definite treatment with a definite aim in view; he adds to it and subtracts from it, emphasizing one effect, toning down another, laying on a touch of colour here, another there, all the time carefully considering the over-all result and paying strict attention to the laws of form and style. He exercises the keenest judgment and chooses his words with complete freedom. His material is entirely subordinated to his artistic purpose; he wants to express this and nothing else. He is wholly at one with the creative process, no matter whether he has deliberately made himself its spearhead, as it were, or whether it has made him its instrument so completely that he has lost all consciousness of this fact. In either case, the artist is so identified with his work that his intentions and his faculties are indistinguishable from the act of creation itself. There is no need, I think, to give examples of this from the history of literature or from the testimony of the artists themselves.

110   Nor need I cite examples of the other class of works which flow more or less complete and perfect from the author's pen.

They come as it were fully arrayed into the world, as Pallas Athene sprang from the head of Zeus. These works positively force themselves upon the author; his hand is seized, his pen writes things that his mind contemplates with amazement. The work brings with it its own form; anything he wants to add is rejected, and what he himself would like to reject is thrust back at him. While his conscious mind stands amazed and empty before this phenomenon, he is overwhelmed by a flood of thoughts and images which he never intended to create and which his own will could never have brought into being. Yet in spite of himself he is forced to admit that it is his own self speaking, his own inner nature revealing itself and uttering things which he would never have entrusted to his tongue. He can only obey the apparently alien impulse within him and follow where it leads, sensing that his work is greater than himself, and wields a power which is not his and which he cannot command. Here the artist is not identical with the process of creation; he is aware that he is subordinate to his work or stands outside it, as though he were a second person; or as though a person other than himself had fallen within the magic circle of an alien will.

111 So when we discuss the psychology of art, we must bear in mind these two entirely different modes of creation, for much that is of the greatest importance in judging a work of art depends on this distinction. It is one that had been sensed earlier by Schiller, who as we know attempted to classify it in his concept of the *sentimental* and the *naïve*. The psychologist would call "sentimental" art *introverted* and the "naïve" kind *extraverted*. The introverted attitude is characterized by the subject's assertion of his conscious intentions and aims against the demands of the object, whereas the extraverted attitude is characterized by the subject's subordination to the demands which the object makes upon him. In my view, Schiller's plays and most of his poems give one a good idea of the introverted attitude: the material is mastered by the conscious intentions of the poet. The extraverted attitude is illustrated by the second part of *Faust*: here the material is distinguished by its refractoriness. A still more striking example is Nietzsche's *Zarathustra*, where the author himself observed how "one became two."

112 From what I have said, it will be apparent that a shift of psychological standpoint has taken place as soon as one speaks

not of the poet as a person but of the creative process that moves him. When the focus of interest shifts to the latter, the poet comes into the picture only as a reacting subject. This is immediately evident in our second category of works, where the consciousness of the poet is not identical with the creative process. But in works of the first category the opposite appears to hold true. Here the poet appears to be the creative process itself, and to create of his own free will without the slightest feeling of compulsion. He may even be fully convinced of his freedom of action and refuse to admit that his work could be anything else than the expression of his will and ability.

113   Here we are faced with a question which we cannot answer from the testimony of the poets themselves. It is really a scientific problem that psychology alone can solve. As I hinted earlier, it might well be that the poet, while apparently creating out of himself and producing what he consciously intends, is nevertheless so carried away by the creative impulse that he is no longer aware of an "alien" will, just as the other type of poet is no longer aware of his own will speaking to him in the apparently "alien" inspiration, although this is manifestly the voice of his own self. The poet's conviction that he is creating in absolute freedom would then be an illusion: he fancies he is swimming, but in reality an unseen current sweeps him along.

114   This is not by any means an academic question, but is supported by the evidence of analytical psychology. Researches have shown that there are all sorts of ways in which the conscious mind is not only influenced by the unconscious but actually guided by it. Yet is there any evidence for the supposition that a poet, despite his self-awareness, may be taken captive by his work? The proof may be of two kinds, direct or indirect. Direct proof would be afforded by a poet who thinks he knows what he is saying but actually says more than he is aware of. Such cases are not uncommon. Indirect proof would be found in cases where behind the apparent free will of the poet there stands a higher imperative that renews its peremptory demands as soon as the poet voluntarily gives up his creative activity, or that produces psychic complications whenever his work has to be broken off against his will.

115   Analysis of artists consistently shows not only the strength of

the creative impulse arising from the unconscious, but also its capricious and wilful character. The biographies of great artists make it abundantly clear that the creative urge is often so imperious that it battens on their humanity and yokes everything to the service of the work, even at the cost of health and ordinary human happiness. The unborn work in the psyche of the artist is a force of nature that achieves its end either with tyrannical might or with the subtle cunning of nature herself, quite regardless of the personal fate of the man who is its vehicle. The creative urge lives and grows in him like a tree in the earth from which it draws its nourishment. We would do well, therefore, to think of the creative process as a living thing implanted in the human psyche. In the language of analytical psychology this living thing is an *autonomous complex*. It is a split-off portion of the psyche, which leads a life of its own outside the hierarchy of consciousness. Depending on its energy charge, it may appear either as a mere disturbance of conscious activities or as a supraordinate authority which can harness the ego to its purpose. Accordingly, the poet who identifies with the creative process would be one who acquiesces from the start when the unconscious imperative begins to function. But the other poet, who feels the creative force as something alien, is one who for various reasons cannot acquiesce and is thus caught unawares.

116   It might be expected that this difference in its origins would be perceptible in a work of art. For in the one case it is a conscious product shaped and designed to have the effect intended. But in the other we are dealing with an event originating in unconscious nature; with something that achieves its aim without the assistance of human consciousness, and often defies it by wilfully insisting on its own form and effect. We would therefore expect that works belonging to the first class would nowhere overstep the limits of comprehension, that their effect would be bounded by the author's intention and would not extend beyond it. But with works of the other class we would have to be prepared for something suprapersonal that transcends our understanding to the same degree that the author's consciousness was in abeyance during the process of creation. We would expect a strangeness of form and content, thoughts that can only be apprehended intuitively, a language pregnant with meanings, and

images that are true symbols because they are the best possible expressions for something unknown—bridges thrown out towards an unseen shore.

117   These criteria are, by and large, corroborated in practice. Whenever we are confronted with a work that was consciously planned and with material that was consciously selected, we find that it agrees with the first class of qualities, and in the other case with the second. The example we gave of Schiller's plays, on the one hand, and *Faust II* on the other, or better still *Zarathustra,* is an illustration of this. But I would not undertake to place the work of an unknown poet in either of these categories without first having examined rather closely his personal relations with his work. It is not enough to know whether the poet belongs to the introverted or to the extraverted type, since it is possible for either type to work with an introverted attitude at one time, and an extraverted attitude at another. This is particularly noticeable in the difference between Schiller's plays and his philosophical writings, between Goethe's perfectly formed poems and the obvious struggle with his material in *Faust II,* and between Nietzsche's well-turned aphorisms and the rushing torrent of *Zarathustra.* The same poet can adopt different attitudes to his work at different times, and on this depends the standard we have to apply.

118   The question, as we now see, is exceedingly complicated, and the complication grows even worse when we consider the case of the poet who identifies with the creative process. For should it turn out that the apparently conscious and purposeful manner of composition is a subjective illusion of the poet, then his work would possess symbolic qualities that are outside the range of his consciousness. They would only be more difficult to detect, because the reader as well would be unable to get beyond the bounds of the poet's consciousness which are fixed by the spirit of the time. There is no Archimedean point outside his world by which he could lift his time-bound consciousness off its hinges and recognize the symbols hidden in the poet's work. For a symbol is the intimation of a meaning beyond the level of our present powers of comprehension.

119   I raise this question only because I do not want my typological classification to limit the possible significance of works of art which apparently mean no more than what they say. But we

have often found that a poet who has gone out of fashion is suddenly rediscovered. This happens when our conscious development has reached a higher level from which the poet can tell us something new. It was always present in his work but was hidden in a symbol, and only a renewal of the spirit of the time permits us to read its meaning. It needed to be looked at with fresher eyes, for the old ones could see in it only what they were accustomed to see. Experiences of this kind should make us cautious, as they bear out my earlier argument. But works that are openly symbolic do not require this subtle approach; their pregnant language cries out at us that they mean more than they say. We can put our finger on the symbol at once, even though we may not be able to unriddle its meaning to our entire satisfaction. A symbol remains a perpetual challenge to our thoughts and feelings. That probably explains why a symbolic work is so stimulating, why it grips us so intensely, but also why it seldom affords us a purely aesthetic enjoyment. A work that is manifestly not symbolic appeals much more to our aesthetic sensibility because it is complete in itself and fulfils its purpose.

120   What then, you may ask, can analytical psychology contribute to our fundamental problem, which is the mystery of artistic creation? All that we have said so far has to do only with the psychological phenomenology of art. Since nobody can penetrate to the heart of nature, you will not expect psychology to do the impossible and offer a valid explanation of the secret of creativity. Like every other science, psychology has only a modest contribution to make towards a deeper understanding of the phenomena of life, and is no nearer than its sister sciences to absolute knowledge.

121   We have talked so much about the meaning of works of art that one can hardly suppress a doubt as to whether art really "means" anything at all. Perhaps art has no "meaning," at least not as we understand meaning. Perhaps it is like nature, which simply *is* and "means" nothing beyond that. Is "meaning" necessarily more than mere interpretation—an interpretation secreted into something by an intellect hungry for meaning? Art, it has been said, is beauty, and "a thing of beauty is a joy for ever." It needs no meaning, for meaning has nothing to do with art. Within the sphere of art, I must accept the truth of this statement. But when I speak of the relation of psychology to art

77

we are outside its sphere, and it is impossible for us not to specu-
late. We must interpret, we must find meanings in things, otherwise we would be quite unable to think about them. We have to
break down life and events, which are self-contained processes,
into meanings, images, concepts, well knowing that in doing so
we are getting further away from the living mystery. As long as
we ourselves are caught up in the process of creation, we neither
see nor understand; indeed we ought not to understand, for
nothing is more injurious to immediate experience than cognition. But for the purpose of cognitive understanding we must
detach ourselves from the creative process and look at it from
the outside; only then does it become an image that expresses
what we are bound to call "meaning." What was a mere phenomenon before becomes something that in association with
other phenomena has meaning, that has a definite role to play,
serves certain ends, and exerts meaningful effects. And when we
have seen all this we get the feeling of having understood and
explained something. In this way we meet the demands of science.

122   When, a little earlier, we spoke of a work of art as a tree
growing out of the nourishing soil, we might equally well have
compared it to a child growing in the womb. But as all compari-
sons are lame, let us stick to the more precise terminology of
science. You will remember that I described the nascent work in
the psyche of the artist as an autonomous complex. By this we
mean a psychic formation that remains subliminal until its
energy-charge is sufficient to carry it over the threshold into consciousness. Its association with consciousness does not mean that
it is assimilated, only that it is perceived; but it is not subject to
conscious control, and can be neither inhibited nor voluntarily
reproduced. Therein lies the autonomy of the complex: it appears and disappears in accordance with its own inherent tendencies, independently of the conscious will. The creative
complex shares this peculiarity with every other autonomous
complex. In this respect it offers an analogy with pathological
processes, since these too are characterized by the presence of
autonomous complexes, particularly in the case of mental disturbances. The divine frenzy of the artist comes perilously close
to a pathological state, though the two things are not identical.
The *tertium comparationis* is the autonomous complex. But the

presence of autonomous complexes is not in itself pathological, since normal people, too, fall temporarily or permanently under their domination. This fact is simply one of the normal peculiarities of the psyche, and for a man to be unaware of the existence of an autonomous complex merely betrays a high degree of unconsciousness. Every typical attitude that is to some extent differentiated shows a tendency to become an autonomous complex, and in most cases it actually does. Again, every instinct has more or less the character of an autonomous complex. In itself, therefore, an autonomous complex has nothing morbid about it; only when its manifestations are frequent and disturbing is it a symptom of illness.

123   How does an autonomous complex arise? For reasons which we cannot go into here, a hitherto unconscious portion of the psyche is thrown into activity, and gains ground by activating the adjacent areas of association. The energy needed for this is naturally drawn from consciousness—unless the latter happens to identify with the complex. But where this does not occur, the drain of energy produces what Janet calls an *abaissement du niveau mental*. The intensity of conscious interests and activities gradually diminishes, leading either to apathy—a condition very common with artists—or to a regressive development of the conscious functions, that is, they revert to an infantile and archaic level and undergo something like a degeneration. The "inferior parts of the functions," as Janet calls them, push to the fore; the instinctual side of the personality prevails over the ethical, the infantile over the mature, and the unadapted over the adapted. This too is something we see in the lives of many artists. The autonomous complex thus develops by using the energy that has been withdrawn from the conscious control of the personality.

124   But in what does an autonomous *creative* complex consist? Of this we can know next to nothing so long as the artist's work affords us no insight into its foundations. The work presents us with a finished picture, and this picture is amenable to analysis only to the extent that we can recognize it as a symbol. But if we are unable to discover any symbolic value in it, we have merely established that, so far as we are concerned, it means no more than what it says, or to put it another way, that it *is* no more than what it *seems* to be. I use the word "seems" because our own bias may prevent a deeper appreciation of it. At any rate we

can find no incentive and no starting-point for an analysis. But in the case of a symbolic work we should remember the dictum of Gerhard Hauptmann: "Poetry evokes out of words the resonance of the primordial word." The question we should ask, therefore, is: "What primordial image lies behind the imagery of art?"

125   This question needs a little elucidation. I am assuming that the work of art we propose to analyse, as well as being symbolic, has its source not in the *personal unconscious* of the poet, but in a sphere of unconscious mythology whose primordial images are the common heritage of mankind. I have called this sphere the *collective unconscious,* to distinguish it from the personal unconscious. The latter I regard as the sum total of all those psychic processes and contents which are capable of becoming conscious and often do, but are then suppressed because of their incompatibility and kept subliminal. Art receives tributaries from this sphere too, but muddy ones; and their predominance, far from making a work of art a symbol, merely turns it into a symptom. We can leave this kind of art without injury and without regret to the purgative methods employed by Freud.

126   In contrast to the personal unconscious, which is a relatively thin layer immediately below the threshold of consciousness, the collective unconscious shows no tendency to become conscious under normal conditions, nor can it be brought back to recollection by any analytical technique,[2] since it was never repressed or forgotten. The collective unconscious is not to be thought of as a self-subsistent entity; it is no more than a potentiality handed down to us from primordial times in the specific form of mnemonic images[3] or inherited in the anatomical structure of

2 [By this Jung probably meant the analytical techniques that were in use at the time (1922), and more particularly the Freudian. Whether he had by then developed his own technique for constellating the collective unconscious is an open question. Cf. "The Transcendent Function" (orig. 1916), pp. 67ff., and ch. VI of Jung's *Memories, Dreams, Reflections.*—EDITORS.]

3 [Here Jung defines the *collective unconscious* in much the same way as a year earlier (*Psychological Types*, pars. 624, 747) he had defined the *archetype*. Still earlier, in 1919, using the term "archetype" for the first time, he had stated: "The instincts and the archetypes together form the 'collective unconscious'" ("Instinct and the Unconscious," par. 270). This is in better agreement with his later formulations. The subject of the above sentence should therefore be understood as the archetype.—EDITORS.]

the brain. There are no inborn ideas, but there are inborn possibilities of ideas that set bounds to even the boldest fantasy and keep our fantasy activity within certain categories: *a priori* ideas, as it were, the existence of which cannot be ascertained except from their effects. They appear only in the shaped material of art as the regulative principles that shape it; that is to say, only by inferences drawn from the finished work can we reconstruct the age-old original [4] of the primordial image.

127   The primordial image, or archetype, is a figure—be it a daemon, a human being, or a process—that constantly recurs in the course of history and appears wherever creative fantasy is freely expressed. Essentially, therefore, it is a mythological figure. When we examine these images more closely, we find that they give form to countless typical experiences of our ancestors. They are, so to speak, the psychic residua of innumerable experiences of the same type. They present a picture of psychic life in the average, divided up and projected into the manifold figures of the mythological pantheon. But the mythological figures are themselves products of creative fantasy and still have to be translated into conceptual language. Only the beginnings of such a language exist, but once the necessary concepts are created they could give us an abstract, scientific understanding of the unconscious processes that lie at the roots of the primordial images. In each of these images there is a little piece of human psychology and human fate, a remnant of the joys and sorrows that have been repeated countless times in our ancestral history, and on the average follow ever the same course. It is like a deeply graven river-bed in the psyche, in which the waters of life, instead of flowing along as before in a broad but shallow stream, suddenly swell into a mighty river. This happens whenever that particular set of circumstances is encountered which over long periods of time has helped to lay down the primordial image.

128   The moment when this mythological situation reappears is always characterized by a peculiar emotional intensity; it is as though chords in us were struck that had never resounded before, or as though forces whose existence we never suspected were unloosed. What makes the struggle for adaptation so labo-

---

[4] [Lit., "primitive Vorlage." In the light of Jung's later formulations, this would mean the "archetype *per se*" as distinct from the "archetypal image." Cf. particularly "On the Nature of the Psyche," par. 417.—EDITORS.]

rious is the fact that we have constantly to be dealing with individual and atypical situations. So it is not surprising that when an archetypal situation occurs we suddenly feel an extraordinary sense of release, as though transported, or caught up by an overwhelming power. At such moments we are no longer individuals, but the race; the voice of all mankind resounds in us. The individual man cannot use his powers to the full unless he is aided by one of those collective representations we call ideals, which releases all the hidden forces of instinct that are inaccessible to his conscious will. The most effective ideals are always fairly obvious variants of an archetype, as is evident from the fact that they lend themselves to allegory. The ideal of the "mother country," for instance, is an obvious allegory of the mother, as is the "fatherland" of the father. Its power to stir us does not derive from the allegory, but from the symbolical value of our native land. The archetype here is the *participation mystique* of primitive man with the soil on which he dwells, and which contains the spirits of his ancestors.

129   The impact of an archetype, whether it takes the form of immediate experience or is expressed through the spoken word, stirs us because it summons up a voice that is stronger than our own. Whoever speaks in primordial images speaks with a thousand voices; he enthrals and overpowers, while at the same time he lifts the idea he is seeking to express out of the occasional and the transitory into the realm of the ever-enduring. He transmutes our personal destiny into the destiny of mankind, and evokes in us all those beneficent forces that ever and anon have enabled humanity to find a refuge from every peril and to outlive the longest night.

130   That is the secret of great art, and of its effect upon us. The creative process, so far as we are able to follow it at all, consists in the unconscious activation of an archetypal image, and in elaborating and shaping this image into the finished work. By giving it shape, the artist translates it into the language of the present, and so makes it possible for us to find our way back to the deepest springs of life. Therein lies the social significance of art: it is constantly at work educating the spirit of the age, conjuring up the forms in which the age is most lacking. The unsatisfied yearning of the artist reaches back to the primordial image in the unconscious which is best fitted to compensate the

inadequacy and one-sidedness of the present. The artist seizes on this image, and in raising it from deepest unconsciousness he brings it into relation with conscious values, thereby transforming it until it can be accepted by the minds of his contemporaries according to their powers.

131   Peoples and times, like individuals, have their own characteristic tendencies and attitudes. The very word "attitude" betrays the necessary bias that every marked tendency entails. Direction implies exclusion, and exclusion means that very many psychic elements that could play their part in life are denied the right to exist because they are incompatible with the general attitude. The normal man can follow the general trend without injury to himself; but the man who takes to the back streets and alleys because he cannot endure the broad highway will be the first to discover the psychic elements that are waiting to play their part in the life of the collective. Here the artist's relative lack of adaptation turns out to his advantage; it enables him to follow his own yearnings far from the beaten path, and to discover what it is that would meet the unconscious needs of his age. Thus, just as the one-sidedness of the individual's conscious attitude is corrected by reactions from the unconscious, so art represents a process of self-regulation in the life of nations and epochs.

132   I am aware that in this lecture I have only been able to sketch out my views in the barest outline. But I hope that what I have been obliged to omit, that is to say their practical application to poetic works of art, has been furnished by your own thoughts, thus giving flesh and blood to my abstract intellectual frame.

PSYCHOLOGY AND LITERATURE [1]

Introduction

Psychology, which once eked out a modest existence in a small and highly academic backroom, has, in fulfilment of Nietzsche's prophecy, developed in the last few decades into an object of public interest which has burst the framework assigned to it by the universities. In the form of psychotechnics it makes its voice heard in industry, in the form of psychotherapy it has invaded wide areas of medicine, in the form of philosophy it has carried forward the legacy of Schopenhauer and von Hartmann, it has quite literally rediscovered Bachofen and Carus, through it mythology and the psychology of primitives have acquired a new focus of interest, it will revolutionize the science of comparative religion, and not a few theologians want to apply it even to the cure of souls. Will Nietzsche be proved right in the end with his "scientia ancilla psychologiae"?

At present, unfortunately, this encroaching advance of psychology is still a welter of chaotic cross-currents, each of the conflicting schools attempting to cover up the confusion by an all the more vociferous dogmatism and a fanatical defence of its own standpoint. Equally onesided are the attempts to open up all these different areas of knowledge and life to psychological research. Onesidedness and rigidity of principle are, however, the childish errors of every young science that has to perform pioneer work with but few intel-

1 [First published as "Psychologie und Dichtung" in *Philosophie der Literaturwissenschaft* (Berlin, 1930), ed. by Emil Ermatinger; expanded and revised in *Gestaltungen des Unbewussten* (Zurich, 1950). The original version was translated by Eugene Jolas as "Psychology and Poetry," *transition: An International Quarterly for Creative Experiment*, no. 19/20 (June, 1930); also translated by W. S. Dell and Cary F. Baynes, in *Modern Man in Search of a Soul* (London and New York, 1933).

A typescript of an introduction was found among Jung's posthumous papers; it is first published here, in translation. Evidently Jung used the introduction when he read the essay as a lecture, though nothing certain is known of such an occasion. Cf. p. 132, par. (1).—EDITORS.]

lectual tools. Despite all [my] tolerance and realization of the necessity of doctrinal opinions of various kinds, I have never wearied of emphasizing that onesidedness and dogmatism harbour in themselves the gravest dangers precisely in the domain of psychology. The psychologist should constantly bear in mind that his hypothesis is no more at first than the expression of his own subjective premise and can therefore never lay immediate claim to general validity. What the individual researcher has to contribute in explanation of any one of the countless aspects of the psyche is merely a point of view, and it would be doing the grossest violence to the object of research if he tried to make this one point of view into a generally binding truth. The phenomenology of the psyche is so colourful, so variegated in form and meaning, that we cannot possibly reflect all its riches in *one* mirror. Nor in our description of it can we ever embrace the whole, but must be content to shed light only on single parts of the total phenomenon.

Since it is a characteristic of the psyche not only to be the source of all productivity but, more especially, to express itself in all the activities and achievements of the human mind, we can nowhere grasp the nature of the psyche *per se* but can meet it only in its various manifestations. The psychologist is therefore obliged to make himself familiar with a wide range of subjects, not out of presumption and inquisitiveness but rather from love of knowledge, and for this purpose he must abandon his thickly walled specialist fortress and set out on the quest for truth. He will not succeed in banishing the psyche to the confines of the laboratory or of the consulting room, but must follow it through all those realms where its visible manifestations are to be found, however strange they may be to him.

Thus it comes that I, unperturbed by the fact that I am by profession a doctor, speak to you today as a psychologist about the poetic imagination, although this constitutes the proper province of literary science and of aesthetics. On the other hand, it is also a psychic phenomenon, and as such it probably must be taken into account by the psychologist. In so doing I shall not encroach on the territory either of the literary historian or of the aesthetician, for nothing is further from my intentions than to replace their points of view by psychological ones. Indeed, I would be making myself guilty of that same sin of onesidedness which I have just censured. Nor shall I presume to put before you a complete theory of poetic creativity, as that would be altogether impossible for me. My observations should be taken as nothing more than points of view by which a psychological approach to poetry might be oriented in a general way.

———

85

133   It is obvious enough that psychology, being a study of psychic processes, can be brought to bear on the study of literature, for the human psyche is the womb of all the arts and sciences. The investigation of the psyche should therefore be able on the one hand to explain the psychological structure of a work of art, and on the other to reveal the factors that make a person artistically creative. The psychologist is thus faced with two separate and distinct tasks, and must approach them in radically different ways.

134   In the case of a work of art we are confronted with a product of complicated psychic activities—but a product that is apparently intentional and consciously shaped. In the case of the artist we must deal with the psychic apparatus itself. In the first instance the object of analysis and interpretation is a concrete artistic achievement, while in the second it is the creative human being as a unique personality. Although these two objects are intimately related and even interdependent, neither of them can explain the other. It is of course possible to draw inferences about the artist from the work of art, and *vice versa,* but these inferences are never conclusive. At best they are probably surmises or lucky guesses. A knowledge of Goethe's particular relation to his mother throws some light on Faust's exclamation: "The mothers, the mothers, how eerily it sounds!" But it does not enable us to see how the attachment to his mother could produce the *Faust* drama itself, however deeply we sense the importance of this relationship for Goethe the man from the many telltale traces it has left behind in his work. Nor are we more successful in reasoning in the reverse direction. There is nothing in *The Ring of the Nibelungs* that would lead us to discern or to infer the fact that Wagner had a tendency towards transvestism, even though a secret connection does exist between the heroics of the Nibelungs and a certain pathological effeminacy in the man Wagner. The personal psychology of the artist may explain many aspects of his work, but not the work itself. And if ever it did explain his work successfully, the artist's creativity would be revealed as a mere symptom. This would be detrimental both to the work of art and to its repute.

135   The present state of psychological knowledge does not allow

us to establish those rigorous causal connections in the realm of art which we would expect a science to do. Psychology, after all, is the newest of the sciences. It is only in the realm of the psychophysical instincts and reflexes that we can confidently operate with the concept of causality. From the point where true psychic life begins—that is, at a level of greater complexity—the psychologist must content himself with widely ranging descriptions of psychic processes, and with portraying as vividly as he can the warp and woof of the mind in all its amazing intricacy. At the same time, he should refrain from calling any one of these processes "necessary" in the sense that it is causally determined. If the psychologist were able to demonstrate definite causalities in a work of art and in the process of artistic creation, he would leave aesthetics no ground to stand on and would reduce it to a special branch of his own science. Although he should never abandon his claim to investigate and establish the causality of complex psychic processes—to do so would be to deny psychology the right to exist—he will never be able to make good this claim in the fullest sense, because the creative urge which finds its clearest expression in art is irrational and will in the end make a mock of all our rationalistic undertakings. All conscious psychic processes may well be causally explicable; but the creative act, being rooted in the immensity of the unconscious, will forever elude our attempts at understanding. It describes itself only in its manifestations; it can be guessed at, but never wholly grasped. Psychology and aesthetics will always have to turn to one another for help, and the one will not invalidate the other. It is an important principle of psychology that any given psychic material can be shown to derive from causal antecedents; it is a principle of aesthetics that a psychic product can be regarded as existing in and for itself. Whether the work of art or the artist himself is in question, both principles are valid in spite of their relativity.

1. *The Work of Art*

¹³⁶ There is a fundamental difference of attitude between the psychologist's approach to a literary work and that of a literary critic. What is of decisive importance and value for the latter may be quite irrelevant for the former. Indeed, literary products

of highly dubious merit are often of the greatest interest to the psychologist. The so-called "psychological novel" is by no means as rewarding for the psychologist as the literary-minded suppose. Considered as a self-contained whole, such a novel explains itself. It has done its own work of psychological interpretation, and the psychologist can at most criticize or enlarge upon this.

137   In general, it is the non-psychological novel that offers the richest opportunities for psychological elucidation. Here the author, having no intentions of this sort, does not show his characters in a psychological light and thus leaves room for analysis and interpretation, or even invites it by his unprejudiced mode of presentation. Good examples of such novels are those of Benoît, or English fiction after the manner of Rider Haggard, as well as that most popular article of literary mass-production, the detective story, first exploited by Conan Doyle. I would also include Melville's *Moby Dick,* which I consider to be the greatest American novel, in this broad class of writings. An exciting narrative that is apparently quite devoid of psychological intentions is just what interests the psychologist most of all. Such a tale is constructed against a background of unspoken psychological assumptions, and the more unconscious the author is of them, the more this background reveals itself in unalloyed purity to the discerning eye. In the psychological novel, on the other hand, the author himself makes the attempt to raise the raw material of his work into the sphere of psychological discussion, but instead of illuminating it he merely succeeds in obscuring the psychic background. It is from novels of this sort that the layman gets his "psychology"; whereas novels of the first kind require the psychologist to give them a deeper meaning.

138   I have been speaking in terms of the novel, but what I am discussing is a psychological principle which is not restricted to this form of literature. We meet with it also in poetry, and in *Faust* it is so obvious that it divides the first part from the second. The love-tragedy of Gretchen is self-explanatory; there is nothing the psychologist can add to it that has not already been said in better words by the poet. But the second part cries out for interpretation. The prodigious richness of the imaginative material has so overtaxed, or outstripped, the poet's powers of expression that nothing explains itself any more and every line only makes the reader's need of an interpretation more appar-

ent. *Faust* is perhaps the best illustration of these two extremes in the psychology of art.

139   For the sake of clarity I would like to call the one mode of artistic creation *psychological*,[2] and the other *visionary*. The psychological mode works with materials drawn from man's conscious life—with crucial experiences, powerful emotions, suffering, passion, the stuff of human fate in general. All this is assimilated by the psyche of the poet, raised from the commonplace to the level of poetic experience, and expressed with a power of conviction that gives us a greater depth of human insight by making us vividly aware of those everyday happenings which we tend to evade or to overlook because we perceive them only dully or with a feeling of discomfort. The raw material of this kind of creation is derived from the contents of man's consciousness, from his eternally repeated joys and sorrows, but clarified and transfigured by the poet. There is no work left for the psychologist to do—unless perhaps we expect him to explain why Faust fell in love with Gretchen, or why Gretchen was driven to murder her child. Such themes constitute the lot of humankind; they are repeated millions of times and account for the hideous monotony of the police court and the penal code. No obscurity surrounds them, for they fully explain themselves in their own terms.

140   Countless literary products belong to this class: all the novels dealing with love, the family milieu, crime and society, together with didactic poetry, the greater number of lyrics, and drama both tragic and comic. Whatever artistic form they may take,

---

2 [The designation "psychological" is somewhat confusing in this context because, as the subsequent discussion makes clear, the "visionary" mode deals equally with "psychological" material. Moreover, "psychological" is used in still another sense in pars. 136–37, where the "psychological novel" is contrasted with the "non-psychological novel."

[The term "personalistic" suggests itself as coming closer to defining the material in question, which derives from "the sphere of conscious human experience—from the psychic foreground of life" (par. 140). The term "personalistic" occurs elsewhere in Jung's writings, e.g., in *The Practice of Psychotherapy*, pars. 212 and 381, n. 34. Both times it characterizes a particular kind of psychology. The second instance is the more significant in that "personalistic" is contrasted with "archetypal," and this would appear to be precisely the distinction intended between the two kinds of psychological material and the two modes of artistic creation.—EDITORS.]

their contents always derive from the sphere of conscious human experience—from the psychic foreground of life, we might say. That is why I call this mode of creation "psychological"; it remains within the limits of the psychologically intelligible. Everything it embraces—the experience as well as its artistic expression—belongs to the realm of a clearly understandable psychology. Even the psychic raw material, the experiences themselves, have nothing strange about them; on the contrary, they have been known from the beginning of time—passion and its fated outcome, human destiny and its sufferings, eternal nature with its beauty and horror.

141   The gulf that separates the first from the second part of *Faust* marks the difference between the psychological and the visionary modes of artistic creation. Here everything is reversed. The experience that furnishes the material for artistic expression is no longer familiar. It is something strange that derives its existence from the hinterland of man's mind, as if it had emerged from the abyss of prehuman ages, or from a superhuman world of contrasting light and darkness. It is a primordial experience which surpasses man's understanding and to which in his weakness he may easily succumb. The very enormity of the experience gives it its value and its shattering impact. Sublime, pregnant with meaning, yet chilling the blood with its strangeness, it arises from timeless depths; glamorous, daemonic, and grotesque, it bursts asunder our human standards of value and aesthetic form, a terrifying tangle of eternal chaos, a *crimen laesae majestatis humanae.* On the other hand, it can be a revelation whose heights and depths are beyond our fathoming, or a vision of beauty which we can never put into words. This disturbing spectacle of some tremendous process that in every way transcends our human feeling and understanding makes quite other demands upon the powers of the artist than do the experiences of the foreground of life. These never rend the curtain that veils the cosmos; they do not exceed the bounds of our human capacities, and for this reason they are more readily shaped to the demands of art, however shattering they may be for the individual. But the primordial experiences rend from top to bottom the curtain upon which is painted the picture of an ordered world, and allow a glimpse into the unfathomable abyss of the unborn and of things yet to be. Is it a vision of other worlds, or of the

darknesses of the spirit, or of the primal beginnings of the human psyche? We cannot say that it is any or none of these.

> Formation, transformation,
> Eternal Mind's eternal recreation.

142   We find such a vision in the *Shepherd of Hermas*, in Dante, in the second part of *Faust*, in Nietzsche's Dionysian experience,[3] in Wagner's *Ring, Tristan, Parsifal*, in Spitteler's *Olympian Spring*, in William Blake's paintings and poetry, in the *Hypnerotomachia* of the monk Francesco Colonna,[4] in Jacob Boehme's poetic-philosophic stammerings,[5] and in the magnificent but scurrilous imagery of E. T. A. Hoffmann's tale *The Golden Bowl*.[6] In more restricted and succinct form, this primordial experience is the essential content of Rider Haggard's *She* and *Ayesha*, of Benoît's *L'Atlantide*, of Alfred Kubin's *Die andere Seite*, of Meyrink's *Das grüne Gesicht*, of Goetz's *Das Reich ohne Raum*, and of Barlach's *Der tote Tag*. The list might be greatly extended.

143   In dealing with the psychological mode of creation, we need never ask ourselves what the material consists of or what it means. But this question forces itself upon us when we turn to the visionary mode. We are astonished, confused, bewildered, put on our guard or even repelled;[7] we demand commentaries and explanations. We are reminded of nothing in everyday life, but rather of dreams, night-time fears, and the dark, uncanny recesses of the human mind. The public for the most part repudiates this kind of literature, unless it is crudely sensational, and even the literary critic finds it embarrassing. It is true that Dante and Wagner have made his task somewhat easier for him by disguising the visionary experience in a cloak of historical or mythical events, which are then erroneously taken to be the real subject-matter. In both cases the compelling power and deeper

---

[3] Cf. my essay "Wotan," pars. 375ff.
[4] Recently interpreted along the lines of analytical psychology by Linda Fierz-David, in *The Dream of Poliphilo*.
[5] Some samples of Boehme may be found in my *Psychology and Alchemy*, pars. 214ff., and in "A Study in the Process of Individuation," pars. 533ff., 578ff.
[6] Cf. the detailed study by Aniela Jaffé in *Gestaltungen des Unbewussten*.
[7] One has only to think of James Joyce's *Ulysses*, which is a work of the greatest significance in spite or perhaps because of its nihilistic tendencies.

meaning of the work do not lie in the historical or mythical material, but in the visionary experience it serves to express. Rider Haggard, pardonably enough, is generally regarded as a romantic story-teller, but in his case too the tale is only a means—admittedly a rather lush one—for capturing a meaningful content.

144   It is strange that a deep darkness surrounds the sources of the visionary material. This is the exact opposite of what we find in the psychological mode of creation, and we are led to suspect that this obscurity is not unintentional. We are naturally inclined to suppose, under the influence of Freudian psychology, that some highly personal experiences must lie behind all this phantasmagoric darkness, which would help to explain that strange vision of chaos, and why it sometimes seems as if the poet were intentionally concealing the source of his experience. From here it is only a step to the conjecture that this kind of art is pathological and neurotic, but a step that is justified in so far as the visionary material exhibits peculiarities which are observed in the fantasies of the insane. Conversely, psychotic products often contain a wealth of meaning such as is ordinarily found only in the works of a genius. One will naturally feel tempted to regard the whole phenomenon from the standpoint of pathology and to explain the strange images as substitute figures and attempts at concealment. It is easy enough to suppose that an intimate personal experience underlies the "primordial vision," an experience that cannot be reconciled with morality. It may, for instance, have been a love affair that seemed morally or aesthetically incompatible with the personality as a whole or with the poet's fictitious view of himself. His ego then sought to repress this experience altogether, or at least its salient features, and make it unrecognizable, i.e., unconscious. For this purpose the whole arsenal of pathological fantasy is called into play, and because this manoeuvre is bound to be unsatisfactory, it has to be repeated in an almost endless series of fictions. This would account for the proliferation of monstrous, daemonic, grotesque, and perverse figures, which all act as substitutes for the "unacceptable" reality and at the same time conceal it.

145   Such a view of the poet's psychology has aroused considerable attention and is the only theoretical attempt that has been made so far to give a "scientific" explanation of the sources of visionary material. If I now put forward my own view, I do so

because I assume it is not so well-known, and is less understood, than the one I have just described.

146   The reduction of the vision to a personal experience makes it something unreal and unauthentic—a mere substitute, as we have said. The vision thus loses its primordial quality and becomes nothing but a symptom; the teeming chaos shrinks to the proportions of a psychic disturbance. We feel reassured by this explanation, and turn back to our picture of a well-ordered cosmos. As practical and reasonable human beings, we never expected it to be perfect; we accept these unavoidable imperfections which we call abnormalities and diseases, and take it for granted that human nature is not exempt from them. The frightening revelation of abysses that defy human understanding is dismissed as illusion, and the poet is regarded as the victim and perpetrator of deception. His primordial experience was "human, all too human," so much so that he could not face it and had to conceal its meaning from himself.

147   We should do well, I think, to bear clearly in mind the full consequences of this reduction of art to personal factors, and see where it leads. The truth is that it deflects our attention from the psychology of the work of art and focuses it on the psychology of the artist. The latter presents a problem that cannot be denied, but the work of art exists in its own right and cannot be got rid of by changing it into a personal complex. As to what it means to the artist, whether it is just a game, or a mask, or a source of suffering, or a positive achievement, these are questions which we shall discuss in the next section. Our task for the moment is to interpret the work of art psychologically, and to do this we must take its foundation—the primordial experience—as seriously as we do the experiences underlying personalistic art, which no one doubts are real and important. It is certainly much more difficult to believe that a visionary experience can be real, for it has all the appearance of something that does not fall to the ordinary lot of man. It has about it a fatal suggestion of vague metaphysics, so that we feel obliged to intervene in the name of well-intentioned reasonableness. We are driven to the conclusion that such things simply cannot be taken seriously, or else the world would sink back into benighted superstition. Anyone who does not have distinct leanings towards the occult will be inclined to dismiss visionary experiences as "lively fan-

93

tasy" or "poetic licence." The poets themselves contribute to this by putting a wholesome distance between themselves and their work. Spitteler, for example, maintained that his *Olympian Spring* "meant" nothing, and that he could just as well have sung: "May is come, tra-la-la-la-la!" Poets are human too, and what they say about their work is often far from being the best word on the subject. It seems as if we have to defend the seriousness of the visionary experience against the personal resistance of the poet himself.

148   In the *Shepherd of Hermas,* the *Divine Comedy,* and *Faust,* we catch echoes of a preliminary love-episode which culminates in a visionary experience. There is no ground for the assumption that the normal, human experience in the first part of *Faust* is repudiated or concealed in the second, or that Goethe was normal at the time when he wrote Part I but in a neurotic state of mind when he wrote Part II. These three works cover a period of nearly two thousand years, and in each of them we find the undisguised personal love-episode not only connected with the weightier visionary experience but actually subordinated to it. This testimony is significant, for it shows that in the work of art (irrespective of the personal psychology of the poet) the vision represents a deeper and more impressive experience than human passion. In works of art of this nature—and we must never confuse them with the artist as a person—it cannot be doubted that the vision is a genuine primordial experience, no matter what the rationalists may say. It is not something derived or secondary, it is not symptomatic of something else, it is a true symbol—that is, an expression for something real but unknown. The love-episode is a real experience really suffered, and so is the vision. It is not for us to say whether its content is of a physical, psychic, or metaphysical nature. In itself it had psychic reality, and this is no less real than physical reality. Human passion falls within the sphere of conscious experience, while the object of the vision lies beyond it. Through our senses we experience the known, but our intuitions point to things that are unknown and hidden, that by their very nature are secret. If ever they become conscious, they are intentionally kept secret and concealed, for which reason they have been regarded from earliest times as mysterious, uncanny, and deceptive. They are hidden

from man, and he hides himself from them out of religious awe, protecting himself with the shield of science and reason. The ordered cosmos he believes in by day is meant to protect him from the fear of chaos that besets him by night—his enlightenment is born of night-fears! What if there were a living agency beyond our everyday human world—something even more purposeful than electrons? Do we delude ourselves in thinking that we possess and control our own psyches, and is what science calls the "psyche" not just a question-mark arbitrarily confined within the skull, but rather a door that opens upon the human world from a world beyond, allowing unknown and mysterious powers to act upon man and carry him on the wings of the night to a more than personal destiny? It even seems as if the love-episode had served as a mere release, or had been unconsciously arranged for a definite purpose, and as if the personal experience were only a prelude to the all-important "divine comedy."

149   The creator of this kind of art is not the only one who is in touch with the night-side of life; prophets and seers are nourished by it too. St. Augustine says: "And higher still we soared, thinking in our minds and speaking and marvelling at Your works: and so we came to our own souls, and went beyond them to reach at last that region of richness unending, where You feed Israel forever with the food of truth . . ." [8] But this same region also has its victims: the great evil-doers and destroyers who darken the face of the times, and the madmen who approach too near to the fire: "Who among us shall dwell with the devouring fire? Who among us shall dwell with everlasting burnings?" [9] It is true indeed that those whom the gods wish to destroy they first make mad. However dark and unconscious this night-world may be, it is not wholly unfamiliar. Man has known it from time immemorial, and for primitives it is a self-evident part of their cosmos. It is only we who have repudiated it because of our fear of superstition and metaphysics, building up in its place an apparently safer and more manageable world of consciousness in which natural law operates like human law in a society. The poet now and then catches sight of the figures that people the night-world—spirits, demons, and gods; he feels the secret quick-

8 *Confessions* (trans. Sheed), p. 158.
9 Isaiah 33:14.

ening of human fate by a suprahuman design, and has a present-iment of incomprehensible happenings in the pleroma. In short, he catches a glimpse of the psychic world that terrifies the primi-tive and is at the same time his greatest hope. It would, inciden-tally, be an interesting subject for research to investigate how far our recently invented fear of superstition and our materialistic outlook are derived from, and are a further development of, primitive magic and the fear of ghosts. At any rate the fascina-tion exerted by depth psychology and the equally violent resist-ance it evokes are not without relevance to our theme.

150   From the very beginnings of human society we find traces of man's efforts to banish his dark forebodings by expressing them in a magical or propitiatory form. Even in the Rhodesian rock-drawings of the Stone Age there appears, side by side with amaz-ingly lifelike pictures of animals, an abstract pattern—a double cross contained in a circle. This design has turned up in practi-cally every culture, and we find it today not only in Christian churches but in Tibetan monasteries as well. It is the so-called sun-wheel, and since it dates from a time when the wheel had not yet been invented, it cannot have had its origin in any expe-rience of the external world. It is rather a symbol for some inner experience, and as a representation of this it is probably just as lifelike as the famous rhinoceros with tick-birds on its back. There has never been a primitive culture that did not possess a highly developed system of secret teaching, a body of lore con-cerning the things that lie beyond man's earthly existence, and of wise rules of conduct.[10] The men's councils and the totem clans preserve this knowledge, and it is handed down to the younger men in the rites of initiation. The mysteries of the Graeco-Roman world performed the same function, which has left behind a rich deposit in the world's mythologies.

151   It is therefore to be expected that the poet will turn to myth-ological figures in order to give suitable expression to his experi-ence. Nothing would be more mistaken than to suppose that he is working with second-hand material. On the contrary, the pri-mordial experience is the source of his creativeness, but it is so dark and amorphous that it requires the related mythological imagery to give it form. In itself it is wordless and imageless, for

[10] *Die Stammeslehren der Dschagga,* edited by Bruno Gutmann, comprises no less than three volumes and runs to 1975 pages!

it is a vision seen "as in a glass, darkly." It is nothing but a tremendous intuition striving for expression. It is like a whirlwind that seizes everything within reach and assumes visible form as it swirls upward. Since the expression can never match the richness of the vision and can never exhaust its possibilities, the poet must have at his disposal a huge store of material if he is to communicate even a fraction of what he has glimpsed, and must make use of difficult and contradictory images in order to express the strange paradoxes of his vision. Dante decks out his experience in all the imagery of heaven, purgatory, and hell; Goethe brings in the Blocksberg and the Greek underworld; Wagner needs the whole corpus of Nordic myth, including the Parsifal saga; Nietzsche resorts to the hieratic style of the bard and legendary seer; Blake presses into his service the phantasmagoric world of India, the Old Testament, and the Apocalypse; and Spitteler borrows old names for the new figures that pour in alarming profusion from his muse's cornucopia. Nothing is missing in the whole gamut that ranges from the ineffably sublime to the perversely grotesque.

152   The psychologist can do little to elucidate this variegated spectacle except provide comparative material and a terminology for its discussion. Thus, what appears in the vision is the imagery of the collective unconscious. This is the matrix of consciousness and has its own inborn structure. According to phylogenetic law, the psychic structure must, like the anatomical, show traces of the earlier stages of evolution it has passed through. This is in fact so in the case of the unconscious, for in dreams and mental disturbances psychic products come to the surface which show all the traits of primitive levels of development, not only in their form but also in their content and meaning, so that we might easily take them for fragments of esoteric doctrines. Mythological motifs frequently appear, but clothed in modern dress; for instance, instead of the eagle of Zeus, or the great roc, there is an airplane; the fight with the dragon is a railway smash; the dragon-slaying hero is an operatic tenor; the Earth Mother is a stout lady selling vegetables; the Pluto who abducts Persephone is a reckless chauffeur, and so on. What is of particular importance for the study of literature, however, is that the manifestations of the collective unconscious are compensatory to the conscious attitude, so that they have the effect

of bringing a one-sided, unadapted, or dangerous state of consciousness back into equilibrium. This function can also be observed in the symptomatology of neurosis and in the delusions of the insane, where the process of compensation is often perfectly obvious—for instance in the case of people who have anxiously shut themselves off from the world and suddenly discover that their most intimate secrets are known and talked about by everybody. The compensation is, of course, not always as crass as this; with neurotics it is much more subtle, and in dreams—particularly in one's own dreams—it is often a complete mystery at first not only to the layman but even to the specialist, however staggeringly simple it turns out to be once it has been understood. But, as we know, the simplest things are often the most difficult to understand.

153   If we disregard for the moment the possibility that *Faust* was compensatory to Goethe's conscious attitude, the question that arises is this: in what relation does it stand to the conscious outlook of his time, and can this relation also be regarded as compensatory? Great poetry draws its strength from the life of mankind, and we completely miss its meaning if we try to derive it from personal factors. Whenever the collective unconscious becomes a living experience and is brought to bear upon the conscious outlook of an age, this event is a creative act which is of importance for a whole epoch. A work of art is produced that may truthfully be called a message to generations of men. So *Faust* touches something in the soul of every German, as Jacob Burckhardt has already remarked.[11] So also Dante's fame is immortal, and the *Shepherd of Hermas* was very nearly included in the New Testament canon. Every period has its bias, its particular prejudice, and its psychic malaise. An epoch is like an individual; it has its own limitations of conscious outlook, and therefore requires a compensatory adjustment. This is effected by the collective unconscious when a poet or seer lends expression to the unspoken desire of his times and shows the way, by word or deed, to its fulfilment—regardless whether this blind collective need results in good or evil, in the salvation of an epoch or its destruction.

154   It is always dangerous to speak of one's own times, because

11 Letter to Albert Brenner. [In 1855. See Dru trans. of Burckhardt's letters, p. 116, and Jung, *Symbols of Transformation*, par. 45, n. 45.—EDITORS.]

what is at stake is too vast to be comprehended.[12] A few hints must therefore suffice. Francesco Colonna's book takes the form of a dream which depicts the apotheosis of love. It does not tell the story of a human passion, but describes a relationship to the anima, man's subjective image of woman, incarnated in the fictitious figure of the lady Polia. The relationship is played out in the pagan setting of classical antiquity, and this is remarkable because the author, so far as we know, was a monk. His book, written in 1453, compensates the medieval Christian outlook by conjuring up a simultaneously older and more youthful world from Hades, which is at the same time the grave and the fruitful mother.[13] The *Hypnerotomachia* of Colonna, says Linda Fierz-David, "is the symbol of the living process of growth which had been set going, obscurely and incomprehensibly, in the men of his time, and had made of the Renaissance the beginning of a new era." [14] Already in Colonna's time the Church was being weakened by schisms, and the age of the great voyages and of scientific discovery was dawning. These tensions between the old and the new are symbolized by the paradoxical figure of Polia, the "modern" soul of the monk Francesco Colonna. After three centuries of religious schism and the scientific discovery of the world, Goethe paints a picture of the megalomania that threatens the Faustian man, and attempts to redeem the inhumanity of this figure by uniting him with the Eternal Feminine, the maternal Sophia. She is the highest manifestation of the anima, stripped of the pagan savagery of the nymph Polia. But this compensation of Faust's inhumanity had no lasting effect, for Nietzsche, after proclaiming the death of God, announces the birth of the Superman, who in turn is doomed to destruction. Nietzsche's contemporary, Spitteler, transforms the waxing and waning of the gods into a myth of the seasons. If we compare his *Prometheus and Epimetheus*[15] with the drama that is being enacted on the world stage today, the prophetic significance of the great work of art will become painfully apparent.[16] Each of these poets speaks with the voice of thousands and tens of thousands, foretelling changes in the conscious outlook of his time.

[12] Written in 1929. [13] *The Dream of Poliphilo,* pp. 234ff. [14] Ibid., p. 27.
[15] I am referring to the first version, written in prose.
[16] Cf. *Psychological Types,* pars. 321ff.

2. *The Artist*

155   The secret of creativeness, like that of the freedom of the will, is a transcendental problem which the psychologist cannot answer but can only describe. The creative personality, too, is a riddle we may try to answer in various ways, but always in vain. Nevertheless, modern psychologists have not been deterred from investigating the problem of the artist and his art. Freud thought he had found a key to the work of art by deriving it from the personal experience of the artist.[17] This was a possible approach, for it was conceivable that a work of art might, like a neurosis, be traced back to complexes. It was Freud's great discovery that neuroses have a quite definite psychic cause, and that they originate in real or imagined emotional experiences in early childhood. Some of his followers, in particular Rank and Stekel, adopted a similar approach and arrived at similar results. It is undeniable that the artist's personal psychology may occasionally be traced out in the roots and in the furthest ramifications of his work. This view, that personal factors in many ways determine the artist's choice of material and the form he gives it, is not in itself new. Credit, however, is certainly due to the Freudian school for showing how far-reaching this influence is and the curious analogies to which it gives rise.

156   Freud considers a neurosis to be a substitute for a direct means of gratification. For him it is something inauthentic—a mistake, a subterfuge, an excuse, a refusal to face facts; in short, something essentially negative that should never have been. One hardly dares to put in a good word for a neurosis, since it is apparently nothing but a meaningless and therefore irritating disturbance. By treating a work of art as something that can be analysed in terms of the artist's repressions we bring it into questionable proximity with a neurosis, where, in a sense, it finds itself in good company, for the Freudian method treats religion and philosophy in the same way. No legitimate objection can be raised to this if it is admitted to be no more than an unearthing of those personal determinants without which a work of art is unthinkable. But if it is claimed that such an anal-

17 See his essays on Jensen's *Gradiva* (Standard Edition, IX), and on Leonardo da Vinci (XI).

ysis explains the work of art itself, then a categorical denial is called for. The essence of a work of art is not to be found in the personal idiosyncrasies that creep into it—indeed, the more there are of them, the less it is a work of art—but in its rising above the personal and speaking from the mind and heart of the artist to the mind and heart of mankind. The personal aspect of art is a limitation and even a vice. Art that is only personal, or predominantly so, truly deserves to be treated as a neurosis. When the Freudian school advances the opinion that all artists are undeveloped personalities with marked infantile autoerotic traits, this judgment may be true of the artist as a man, but it is not applicable to the man as an artist. In this capacity he is neither autoerotic, nor heteroerotic, nor erotic in any sense. He is in the highest degree objective, impersonal, and even inhuman—or suprahuman—for as an artist he is nothing but his work, and not a human being.

157   Every creative person is a duality or a synthesis of contradictory qualities. On the one side he is a human being with a personal life, while on the other he is an impersonal creative process. As a human being he may be sound or morbid, and his personal psychology can and should be explained in personal terms. But he can be understood as an artist only in terms of his creative achievement. We should make a great mistake if we reduced the mode of life of an English gentleman, or a Prussian officer, or a cardinal, to personal factors. The gentleman, the officer, and the high ecclesiastic function as impersonal officials, and each role has its own objective psychology. Although the artist is the exact opposite of an official, there is nevertheless a secret analogy between them in so far as a specifically artistic psychology is more collective than personal in character. Art is a kind of innate drive that seizes a human being and makes him its instrument. The artist is not a person endowed with free will who seeks his own ends, but one who allows art to realize its purposes through him. As a human being he may have moods and a will and personal aims, but as an artist he is "man" in a higher sense—he is "collective man," a vehicle and moulder of the unconscious psychic life of mankind. That is his office, and it is sometimes so heavy a burden that he is fated to sacrifice happiness and everything that makes life worth living for the ordinary human being. As K. G. Carus says: "Strange are the ways by

which genius is announced, for what distinguishes so supremely endowed a being is that, for all the freedom of his life and the clarity of his thought, he is everywhere hemmed round and prevailed upon by the Unconscious, the mysterious god within him; so that ideas flow to him—he knows not whence; he is driven to work and to create—he knows not to what end; and is mastered by an impulse for constant growth and development—he knows not whither." [18]

158   In these circumstances it is not at all surprising that the artist is an especially interesting specimen for the critical analysis of the psychologist. His life cannot be otherwise than full of conflicts, for two forces are at war within him: on the one hand the justified longing of the ordinary man for happiness, satisfaction, and security, and on the other a ruthless passion for creation which may go so far as to override every personal desire. If the lives of artists are as a rule so exceedingly unsatisfactory, not to say tragic, it is not because of some sinister dispensation of fate, but because of some inferiority in their personality or an inability to adapt. A person must pay dearly for the divine gift of creative fire. It is as though each of us was born with a limited store of energy. In the artist, the strongest force in his make-up, that is, his creativeness, will seize and all but monopolize this energy, leaving so little over that nothing of value can come of it. The creative impulse can drain him of his humanity to such a degree that the personal ego can exist only on a primitive or inferior level and is driven to develop all sorts of defects—ruthlessness, selfishness ("autoeroticism"), vanity, and other infantile traits. These inferiorities are the only means by which it can maintain its vitality and prevent itself from being wholly depleted. The autoeroticism of certain artists is like that of illegitimate or neglected children who from their earliest years develop bad qualities to protect themselves from the destructive influence of a loveless environment. Such children easily become ruthless and selfish, and later display an invincible egoism by remaining all their lives infantile and helpless or by actively offending against morality and the law. How can we doubt that it is his art that explains the artist, and not the insufficiencies and conflicts of his personal life? These are nothing but the regrettable results of his being an artist, a man upon whom a heavier burden is laid

18 *Psyche*, ed. Ludwig Klages, p. 158.

than upon ordinary mortals. A special ability demands a greater expenditure of energy, which must necessarily leave a deficit on some other side of life.

159   It makes no difference whether the artist knows that his work is generated, grows and matures within him, or whether he imagines that it is his own invention. In reality it grows out of him as a child its mother. The creative process has a feminine quality, and the creative work arises from unconscious depths— we might truly say from the realm of the Mothers. Whenever the creative force predominates, life is ruled and shaped by the unconscious rather than by the conscious will, and the ego is swept along on an underground current, becoming nothing more than a helpless observer of events. The progress of the work becomes the poet's fate and determines his psychology. It is not Goethe that creates *Faust*, but *Faust* that creates Goethe.[19] And what is *Faust*? *Faust* is essentially a symbol. By this I do not mean that it is an allegory pointing to something all too familiar, but the expression of something profoundly alive in the soul of every German, which Goethe helped to bring to birth. Could we conceive of anyone but a German writing *Faust* or *Thus Spake Zarathustra*? Both of them strike a chord that vibrates in the German psyche, evoking a "primordial image," as Burckhardt once called it—the figure of a healer or teacher of mankind, or of a wizard. It is the archetype of the Wise Old Man, the helper and redeemer, but also of the magician, deceiver, corrupter, and tempter. This image has lain buried and dormant in the unconscious since the dawn of history; it is awakened whenever the times are out of joint and a great error deflects society from the right path. For when people go astray they feel the need of a guide or teacher, and even of a physician. The seductive error is like a poison that can also act as a cure, and the shadow of a saviour can turn into a fiendish destroyer. These opposing forces are at work in the mythical healer himself: the physician

19 Eckermann's dream, in which he saw Faust and Mephistopheles falling to earth in the form of a double meteor, recalls the motif of the Dioscuri (cf. the motif of the two friends in my essay "Concerning Rebirth," pp. 135ff.), and this sheds light on an essential characteristic of Goethe's psyche. An especially subtle point here is Eckermann's remark that the swift and horned figure of Mephisto reminded him of Mercurius. This observation is in full accord with the alchemical nature of Goethe's masterpiece. (I have to thank my colleague W. Kranefeldt for refreshing my memory of Eckermann's *Conversations*.)

who heals wounds is himself the bearer of a wound, a classic example being Chiron.[20] In Christianity it is the wound in the side of Christ, the great physician. Faust, characteristically enough, is unwounded, which means that he is untouched by the moral problem. A man can be as high-minded as Faust and as devilish as Mephistopheles if he is able to split his personality into two halves, and only then is he capable of feeling "six thousand feet beyond good and evil." Mephistopheles was cheated of his reward, Faust's soul, and for this he presented a bloody reckoning a hundred years later. But who now seriously believes that poets utter truths that apply to all men? And if they do, in what way would we have to regard the work of art?

160   In itself, an archetype is neither good nor evil. It is morally neutral, like the gods of antiquity, and becomes good or evil only by contact with the conscious mind, or else a paradoxical mixture of both. Whether it will be conducive to good or evil is determined, knowingly or unknowingly, by the conscious attitude. There are many such archetypal images, but they do not appear in the dreams of individuals or in works of art unless they are activated by a deviation from the middle way. Whenever conscious life becomes one-sided or adopts a false attitude, these images "instinctively" rise to the surface in dreams and in the visions of artists and seers to restore the psychic balance, whether of the individual or of the epoch.

161   In this way the work of the artist meets the psychic needs of the society in which he lives, and therefore means more than his personal fate, whether he is aware of it or not. Being essentially the instrument of his work, he is subordinate to it, and we have no right to expect him to interpret it for us. He has done his utmost by giving it form, and must leave the interpretation to others and to the future. A great work of art is like a dream; for all its apparent obviousness it does not explain itself and is always ambiguous. A dream never says "you ought" or "this is the truth." It presents an image in much the same way as nature allows a plant to grow, and it is up to us to draw conclusions. If a person has a nightmare, it means he is either too much given to fear or too exempt from it; if he dreams of a wise old man, it means he is either too much of a pedant or else in need of a teacher. In a subtle way both meanings come to the same thing,

20 Cf. C. Kerényi, *Asklepios*, pp. 78f.

as we realize when we let a work of art act upon us as it acted upon the artist. To grasp its meaning, we must allow it to shape us as it shaped him. Then we also understand the nature of his primordial experience. He has plunged into the healing and redeeming depths of the collective psyche, where man is not lost in the isolation of consciousness and its errors and sufferings, but where all men are caught in a common rhythm which allows the individual to communicate his feelings and strivings to mankind as a whole.

162   This re-immersion in the state of *participation mystique* is the secret of artistic creation and of the effect which great art has upon us, for at that level of experience it is no longer the weal or woe of the individual that counts, but the life of the collective. That is why every great work of art is objective and impersonal, and yet profoundly moving. And that is also why the personal life of the artist is at most a help or a hindrance, but is never essential to his creative task. He may go the way of the Philistine, a good citizen, a fool, or a criminal. His personal career may be interesting and inevitable, but it does not explain his art.

V

"ULYSSES": A MONOLOGUE

―――

PICASSO

"ULYSSES": A MONOLOGUE [1]

163   The Ulysses of my title has to do with James Joyce and not with that shrewd and storm-driven figure of Homer's world who knew how to escape by guile and wily deeds the enmity and vengeance of gods and men, and who after a wearisome voyage returned to hearth and home. Joyce's Ulysses, very much unlike his ancient namesake, is a passive, merely perceiving consciousness, a mere eye, ear, nose, and mouth, a sensory nerve exposed without choice or check to the roaring, chaotic, lunatic cataract of psychic and physical happenings, and registering all this with almost photographic accuracy.

164   *Ulysses* is a book that pours along for seven hundred and thirty-five pages, a stream of time seven hundred and thirty-five days long which all consist in one single and senseless day in the life of every man, the completely irrelevant sixteenth day of June, 1904, in Dublin—a day on which, in all truth, nothing happens. The stream begins in the void and ends in the void. Is all this perhaps one single, immensely long, and excessively

[1] [For the genesis of this essay, see appendix, infra, p. 132. It was first published in the *Europäische Revue* (Berlin), VIII:2/9 (Sept., 1932); reprinted in *Wirklichkeit der Seele* (Zurich, 1934). Translated by W. Stanley Dell in *Spring* (New York), 1949, and in *Nimbus* (London), II:1 (June–Aug., 1952), which translation forms the basis of the present version.

[The quotations from *Ulysses* are in accordance with the 10th printing (Paris, 1928), a copy of which Jung owned and cited, though he evidently (infra, par. 171) had seen *Ulysses* upon its first publication, 1922.—EDITORS.]

[Author's headnote added to version in *Wirklichkeit der Seele:*] This literary essay first appeared in the *Europäische Revue*. It is not a scientific treatise, any more than is my *aperçu* on Picasso. I have included it in the present volume because *Ulysses* is an important "document humain" very characteristic of our time, and because my opinions may show how ideas that play a considerable role in my work can be applied to literary material. My essay lacks not only any scientific but also any didactic intention, and is of interest to the reader only as a subjective confession.

complicated Strindbergian pronouncement upon the essence of human life—a pronouncement which, to the reader's dismay, is never finished? Possibly it does touch upon the essence, but quite certainly it reflects life's ten thousand facets and their hundred thousand gradations of colour. So far as I can see, there are in those seven hundred and thirty-five pages no obvious repetitions, not a single blessed island where the long-suffering reader may come to rest; no place where he can seat himself, drunk with memories, and contemplate with satisfaction the stretch of road he has covered, be it one hundred pages or even less. If only he could spot some little commonplace that had obligingly slipped in again where it was not expected! But no! The pitiless stream rolls on without a break, and its velocity or viscosity increases in the last forty pages till it sweeps away even the punctuation marks. Here the suffocating emptiness becomes so unbearably tense that it reaches the bursting point. This utterly hopeless emptiness is the dominant note of the whole book. It not only begins and ends in nothingness, it consists of nothing but nothingness.[2] It is all infernally nugatory. As a piece of technical virtuosity it is a brilliant and hellish monster-birth.[3]

165   I had an uncle whose thinking was always direct and to the point. One day he stopped me on the street and demanded: "Do you know how the devil tortures the souls in hell?" When I said no, he replied: "He keeps them waiting." And with that he walked away. This remark occurred to me when I was ploughing through *Ulysses* for the first time. Every sentence rouses an expectation that is not fulfilled; finally, out of sheer resignation, you come to expect nothing, and to your horror it gradually dawns on you that you have hit the mark. In actual fact nothing happens, nothing comes of it all,[4] and yet a secret expectation battling with hopeless resignation drags the reader from page to page. The seven hundred and thirty-five pages that contain

[2] As Joyce himself says (*Work in Progress*, in *transition*): "We may come, touch and go, from atoms and ifs but we are presurely destined to be odd's without ends." [As in *Finnegans Wake* (1939), p. 455. Fragments were published 1924–38, under the title *Work in Progress*, in the monthly magazine *transition* and elsewhere.—EDITORS.]

[3] Curtius (*James Joyce und sein Ulysses*) calls *Ulysses* a "Luciferian book, a work of Antichrist."

[4] Curtius (ibid., p. 60): "A metaphysical nihilism is the substance of Joyce's work."

nothing by no means consist of blank paper but are closely printed. You read and read and read and you pretend to understand what you read. Occasionally you drop through an airpocket into a new sentence, but once the proper degree of resignation has been reached you get accustomed to anything. Thus I read to page 135 with despair in my heart, falling asleep twice on the way. The incredible versatility of Joyce's style has a monotonous and hypnotic effect. Nothing comes to meet the reader, everything turns away from him, leaving him gaping after it. The book is always up and away, dissatisfied with itself, ironic, sardonic, virulent, contemptuous, sad, despairing, and bitter. It plays on the reader's sympathies to his own undoing unless sleep kindly intervenes and puts a stop to this drain of energy. Arrived at page 135, after making several heroic efforts to get at the book, to "do it justice," as the phrase goes, I fell at last into profound slumber.[5] When I awoke quite a while later, my views had undergone such a clarification that I started to read the book backwards. This method proved as good as the usual one; the book can just as well be read backwards, for it has no back and no front, no top and no bottom. Everything could easily have happened before, or might have happened afterwards.[6] You can read any of the conversations just as pleasurably backwards, for you don't miss the point of the gags. Every sentence is a gag, but taken together they make no point. You can also stop in the middle of a sentence—the first half still makes sense enough to live by itself, or at least seems to. The

[5] The magic words that sent me to sleep occur at the bottom of p. 134 and top of p. 135: "that stone effigy in frozen music, horned and terrible, of the human form divine, that eternal symbol of wisdom and prophecy which, if aught that the imagination or the hand of sculptor has wrought in marble of soultransfigured and of soultransfiguring deserves to live, deserves to live." At this point, dizzy with sleep, I turned the page and my eye fell on the following passage: "a man supple in combat: stonehorned, stonebearded, heart of stone." This refers to Moses, who refused to be cowed by the might of Egypt. The two passages contained the narcotic that switched off my consciousness, activating a still unconscious train of thought which consciousness would only have disturbed. As I later discovered, it dawned on me here for the first time what the author was doing and what was the idea behind his work.

[6] This is greatly intensified in *Work in Progress*. Carola Giedion-Welcker aptly remarks on the "ever-recurring ideas in ever-changing forms, projected into a sphere of absolute irreality. Absolute time, absolute space" (*Neue Schweizer Rundschau*, Sept. 1929, p. 666).

whole work has the character of a worm cut in half, that can grow a new head or a new tail as required.

166   This singular and uncanny characteristic of the Joycean mind shows that his work pertains to the class of cold-blooded animals and specifically to the worm family. If worms were gifted with literary powers they would write with the sympathetic nervous system for lack of a brain.[7] I suspect that something of this kind has happened to Joyce, that we have here a case of visceral thinking[8] with severe restriction of cerebral activity and its confinement to the perceptual processes. One is driven to unqualified admiration for Joyce's feats in the sensory sphere: what he sees, hears, tastes, smells, touches, inwardly as well as outwardly, is beyond measure astonishing. The ordinary mortal, if he is a specialist in sense-perception, is usually restricted either to the outer world or to the inner. Joyce knows them both. Garlands of subjective association twine themselves about the objective figures on a Dublin street. Objective and subjective, outer and inner, are so constantly intermingled that in the end, despite the clearness of the individual images, one wonders whether one is dealing with a physical or with a transcendental tape worm.[9] The tapeworm is a whole living cosmos in itself and is fabulously procreative; this, it seems to me, is an inelegant but not unfitting image for Joyce's proliferating chapters. It is true that the tapeworm can produce nothing but other tapeworms, but it produces them in inexhaustible quantities.

[7] In Janet's psychology this phenomenon is known as *abaissement du niveau mental*. Among the insane it happens involuntarily, but with Joyce it is the result of deliberate training. All the richness and grotesque profundity of dream-thinking come to the surface when the "fonction du réel," that is, adapted consciousness, is switched off. Hence the predominance of psychic and verbal automatisms and the total neglect of any communicable meaning.

[8] I think Stuart Gilbert (*James Joyce's "Ulysses,"* 1930, p. 40) is right in supposing that each chapter is presided over, among other things, by one of the visceral or sensory dominants. Those he cites are the kidneys, genitals, heart, lungs, oesophagus, brain, blood, ear, musculature, eye, nose, uterus, nerves, skeleton, skin. These dominants each function as a *leitmotif*. My remark about visceral thinking was written in 1930. For me Gilbert's proof offers valuable confirmation of the psychological fact that an *abaissement du niveau mental* constellates what Wernicke calls the "organ-representatives," i.e., symbols representing the organs.

[9] Curtius, p. 30: "He reproduces the stream of consciousness without filtering it either logically or ethically."

Joyce's book might have been fourteen hundred and seventy pages long or even a multiple of that and still it would not have lessened infinity by a drop, and the essential would still have remained unsaid. But does Joyce want to say anything essential? Has this old-fashioned prejudice any right to exist here? Oscar Wilde maintained that a work of art is something entirely useless. Nowadays even the Philistine would raise no objection to this, yet in his heart he still expects a work of art to contain something "essential." Where is it with Joyce? Why doesn't he say it right out? Why doesn't he hand it to the reader with an expressive gesture—"a straight way, so that fools shall not err therein"?

167   Yes, I admit I feel I have been made a fool of. The book would not meet me half way, nothing in it made the least attempt to be agreeable, and that always gives the reader an irritating sense of inferiority. Obviously I have so much of the Philistine in my blood that I am naïve enough to suppose that a book wants to tell me something, to be understood—a sad case of mythological anthropomorphism projected on to the book! And what a book—no opinion possible—epitome of maddening defeat of intelligent reader, who after all is not such a—(if I may use Joyce's suggestive style). Surely a book has a content, represents something; but I suspect that Joyce did not wish to "represent" anything. Does it by any chance represent *him*—does that explain this solipsistic isolation, this drama without eyewitnesses, this infuriating disdain for the assiduous reader? Joyce has aroused my ill will. One should never rub the reader's nose into his own stupidity, but that is just what *Ulysses* does.

168   A therapist like myself is always practising therapy—even on himself. Irritation means: You haven't yet seen what's behind it. Consequently we should follow up our irritation and examine whatever it is we discover in our ill temper. I observe then: this solipsism, this contempt for the cultivated and intelligent member of the reading public who wants to understand,[10] who is well-meaning, and who tries to be kindly and just, gets on my nerves. There we have it, the cold-blooded unrelatedness of his mind which seems to come from the saurian in him or from still lower regions—conversation in and with one's own intestines—a

10 Curtius, p. 8: "The author has done everything to avoid making it easier for the reader to understand."

man of stone, he with the horns of stone, the stony beard, the petrified intestines, Moses, turning his back with stony unconcern on the flesh-pots and gods of Egypt, and also on the reader, thereby outraging his feelings of good will.

169   From this stony underworld there rises up the vision of the tapeworm, rippling, peristaltic, monotonous because of its endless proglottic proliferation. No proglottid is quite like any other, yet they can easily be confused. In every segment of the book, however small, Joyce himself is the sole content of the segment. Everything is new and yet remains what it was from the beginning. Talk of likeness to nature! What pullulating richness—and what boredom! Joyce bores me to tears, but it is a vicious dangerous boredom such as not even the worst banality could induce. It is the boredom of nature, the bleak whistling of the wind over the crags of the Hebrides, sunrise and sunset over the wastes of the Sahara, the roar of the sea—real Wagnerian "programme music" as Curtius rightly says, and yet eternal repetition. Notwithstanding Joyce's baffling many-sidedness, certain themes can be picked out though they may not be intended. Perhaps he would like there to be none, for causality and finality have neither place nor meaning in his world, any more than have values. Nevertheless, themes are unavoidable, they are the scaffolding for all psychic happenings, however hard one tries to soak the soul out of every happening, as Joyce consistently does. Everything is desouled, every particle of warm blood has been chilled, events unroll in icy egoism. In all the book there is nothing pleasing, nothing refreshing, nothing hopeful, but only things that are grey, grisly, gruesome, or pathetic, tragic, ironic, all from the seamy side of life and so chaotic that you have to look for the thematic connections with a magnifying glass. And yet they are there, first of all in the form of unavowed resentments of a highly personal nature, the wreckage of a violently amputated boyhood; then as flotsam from the whole history of thought exhibited in pitiful nakedness to the staring crowd. The religious, erotic, and domestic prehistory of the author is reflected in the drab surface of the stream of events; we even behold the disintegration of his personality into Bloom, *l'homme moyen sensuel,* and the almost gaseous Stephen Dedalus, who is mere speculation and mere mind. Of these two, the former has no son and the latter no father.

170   Somewhere there may be a secret order or parallelism in the chapters—authoritative voices have been raised to this effect[11]—but in any case it is so well concealed that at first I noticed nothing of the kind. And even if I had, it would not have interested me in my helplessly irritated state, any more than would the monotony of any other squalid human comedy.

171   I had already taken up *Ulysses* in 1922 but had laid it aside disappointed and vexed. Today it still bores me as it did then. Why do I write about it? Ordinarily, I would no more be doing this than writing about any other form of surrealism (what is surrealism?) that passes my understanding. I am writing about Joyce because a publisher was incautious enough to ask me what I thought about him, or rather about *Ulysses*,[12] concerning which opinions are notoriously divided. The only thing beyond dispute is that *Ulysses* is a book that has gone through ten printings and that its author is glorified by some and damned by others. He stands in the cross-fire of discussion and is thus a phenomenon which the psychologist should not ignore. Joyce has exerted a very considerable influence on his contemporaries, and it was this fact which first aroused my interest in *Ulysses*. Had this book slipped noiselessly and unsung into the shades of oblivion I would certainly never have dragged it back again; for it annoyed me thoroughly and amused me only a little. Above all, it held over me the threat of boredom because it had only a negative effect on me and I feared it was the product of an author's negative mood.

172   But of course I am prejudiced. I am a psychiatrist, and that implies a professional prejudice with regard to all manifestations of the psyche. I must therefore warn the reader: the tragicomedy of the average man, the cold shadow-side of life, the dull grey of spiritual nihilism are my daily bread. To me they are a tune ground out on a street organ, stale and without charm. Nothing in all this shocks or moves me, for all too often I have to help people out of these lamentable states. I must combat them incessantly and I may only expend my sympathy on people who do not turn their backs on me. *Ulysses* turns its back on me. It is unco-operative, it wants to go on singing its endless tune into endless time—a tune I know to satiety—and to extend to infinity

11 Curtius, Stuart Gilbert, and others.
12 [See the appendix, infra.]

115

its ganglionic rope-ladder of visceral thinking and cerebration reduced to mere sense-perception. It shows no tendency towards reconstruction; indeed, destructiveness seems to have become an end in itself.

173   But that is not the half of it—there is also the symptomatology! It is all too familiar, those interminable ramblings of the insane who have only a fragmentary consciousness and consequently suffer from a complete lack of judgment and an atrophy of all their values. Instead, there is often an intensification of the sense-activities. We find in these writings an acute power of observation, a photographic memory for sense-perceptions, a sensory curiosity directed inwards as well as outwards, the predominance of retrospective themes and resentments, a delirious confusion of the subjective and psychic with objective reality, a method of presentation that takes no account of the reader but indulges in neologisms, fragmentary quotations, sound- and speech-associations, abrupt transitions and hiatuses of thought. We also find an atrophy of feeling[13] that does not shrink from any depth of absurdity or cynicism. Even the layman would have no difficulty in tracing the analogies between *Ulysses* and the schizophrenic mentality. The resemblance is indeed so suspicious that an indignant reader might easily fling the book aside with the diagnosis "schizophrenia." For the psychiatrist the analogy is startling, but he would nevertheless point out that a characteristic mark of the compositions of the insane, namely, the presence of stereotyped expressions, is notably absent. *Ulysses* may be anything, but it is certainly not monotonous in the sense of being repetitious. (This is not a contradiction of what I said earlier; it is impossible to say anything contradictory about *Ulysses*.) The presentation is consistent and flowing, everything is in motion and nothing is fixed. The whole book is borne along on a subterranean current of life that shows singleness of aim and rigorous selectivity, both these being unmistakable proof of the existence of a unified personal will and directed intention. The mental functions are under severe control; they do not manifest themselves in a spontaneous and erratic way. The perceptive functions, that is, sensation and intuition, are given preference throughout, while the discriminative functions, thinking and feeling, are just as consistently suppressed. They ap-

13 Gilbert, p. 2, speaks of a "deliberate deflation of sentiment."

pear merely as mental contents, as objects of perception. There is no relaxing of the general tendency to present a shadow-picture of the mind and the world, in spite of frequent temptations to surrender to a sudden touch of beauty. These are traits not ordinarily found in the insane. There remains, then, the insane person of an uncommon sort. But the psychiatrist has no criteria for judging such a person. What seems to be mental abnormality may be a kind of mental health which is inconceivable to the average understanding; it may even be a disguise for superlative powers of mind.

174   It would never occur to me to class *Ulysses* as a product of schizophrenia. Moreover, nothing would be gained by this label, for we wish to know why *Ulysses* exerts such a powerful influence and not whether its author is a high-grade or a low-grade schizophrenic. *Ulysses* is no more a pathological product than modern art as a whole. It is "cubistic" in the deepest sense because it resolves the picture of reality into an immensely complex painting whose dominant note is the melancholy of abstract objectivity. Cubism is not a disease but a tendency to represent reality in a certain way—and that way may be grotesquely realistic or grotesquely abstract. The clinical picture of schizophrenia is a mere analogy in that the schizophrenic apparently has the same tendency to treat reality as if it were strange to him, or, conversely, to estrange himself from reality. With the schizophrenic the tendency usually has no recognizable purpose but is a symptom inevitably arising from the disintegration of the personality into fragmentary personalities (the autonomous complexes). In the modern artist it is not produced by any disease in the individual but is a collective manifestation of our time. The artist does not follow an individual impulse, but rather a current of collective life which arises not directly from consciousness but from the collective unconscious of the modern psyche. Just because it is a collective phenomenon it bears identical fruit in the most widely separated realms, in painting as well as literature, in sculpture as well as architecture. It is, moreover, significant that one of the spiritual fathers of the modern movement—van Gogh—was actually schizophrenic.

175   The distortion of beauty and meaning by grotesque objectivity or equally grotesque irreality is, in the insane, a consequence of the destruction of the personality; in the artist it has a

creative purpose. Far from his work being an expression of the destruction of his personality, the modern artist finds the unity of his artistic personality in destructiveness. The Mephistophelian perversion of sense into nonsense, of beauty into ugliness—in such an exasperating way that nonsense almost makes sense and ugliness has a provocative beauty—is a creative achievement that has never been pushed to such extremes in the history of human culture, though it is nothing new in principle. We can observe something similar in the perverse change of style under Ikhnaton, in the inane lamb symbolism of the early Christians, in those doleful Pre-Raphaelite figures, and in late Baroque art, strangling itself in its own convolutions. Despite their differences all these epochs have an inner relationship: they were periods of creative incubation whose meaning cannot be satisfactorily explained from a causal standpoint. Such manifestations of the collective psyche disclose their meaning only when they are considered teleologically as anticipations of something new.

176   The epoch of Ikhnaton was the cradle of the first monotheism, which has been preserved for the world in Jewish tradition. The crude infantilism of the early Christian era portended nothing less than the transformation of the Roman Empire into a City of God. The rejection of the art and science of his time was not an impoverishment for the early Christian, but a great spiritual gain. The Pre-Raphaelite primitives were the heralds of an ideal of bodily beauty that had been lost to the world since classical times. The Baroque was the last of the ecclesiastical styles, and its self-destruction anticipates the triumph of the spirit of science over the spirit of medieval dogmatism. Tiepolo, for instance, who had already reached the danger zone in his technique, is not a symptom of decadence when considered as an artistic personality, but labours with the whole of his being to bring about a much needed disintegration.

177   This being so we can ascribe a positive, creative value and meaning not only to *Ulysses* but also to its artistic congeners. In its destruction of the criteria of beauty and meaning that have held till today, *Ulysses* accomplishes wonders. It insults all our conventional feelings, it brutally disappoints our expectations of sense and content, it thumbs its nose at all synthesis. We would show ill will even to suspect any trace of synthesis or form, for if

we succeeded in demonstrating any such unmodern tendencies in *Ulysses* this would amount to pointing out a gross aesthetic defect. Everything abusive we can say about *Ulysses* bears witness to its peculiar quality, for our abuse springs from the resentment of the unmodern man who does not wish to see what the gods have graciously veiled from sight.

178   All those ungovernable forces that welled up in Nietzsche's Dionysian exuberance and flooded his intellect have burst forth in undiluted form in modern man. Even the darkest passages in the second part of *Faust,* even *Zarathustra* and, indeed, *Ecce Homo,* try in one way or another to recommend themselves to the public. But it is only modern man who has succeeded in creating an art in reverse, a backside of art that makes no attempt to be ingratiating, that tells us just where we get off, speaking with the same rebellious contrariness that had made itself disturbingly felt in those precursors of the moderns (not forgetting Hölderlin) who had already started to topple the old ideals.

179   If we stick to one field of experience only, it is not really possible to see clearly what is happening. It is not a matter of a single thrust aimed at one definite spot, but of an almost universal "restratification" of modern man, who is in the process of shaking off a world that has become obsolete. Unfortunately we cannot see into the future and so we do not know how far we still belong in the deepest sense to the Middle Ages. If, from the watch-towers of the future, we should seem stuck in medievalism up to the ears, I for one would be little surprised. For that alone would satisfactorily explain to us why there should be books or works of art after the style of *Ulysses.* They are drastic purgatives whose full effect would be dissipated if they did not meet with an equally strong and obstinate resistance. They are a kind of psychological specific which is of use only where the hardest and toughest material must be dealt with. They have this in common with Freudian theory, that they undermine with fanatical one-sidedness values that have already begun to crumble.

180   *Ulysses* makes a show of semi-scientific objectivity, at times even employing "scientific" language, and yet it displays a truly unscientific temper: it is sheer negation. Even so it is creative—a creative destruction. Here is no theatrical gesture of a Herostratus burning down temples, but an earnest endeavour to rub the

noses of our contemporaries in the shadow-side of reality, not with any malicious intent but with the guileless naïveté of artistic objectivity. One may safely call the book pessimistic even though at the very end, on nearly the final page, a redeeming light breaks wistfully through the clouds. This is only *one* page against seven hundred and thirty-four which were one and all born of Orcus. Here and there, a fine crystal glitters in the black stream of mud, so that even the unmodern may realize that Joyce is an "artist" who knows his trade—which is more than can be said of most modern artists—and is even a past master at it, but a master who has piously renounced his powers in the name of a higher goal. Even in his "restratification" Joyce has remained a pious Catholic: his dynamite is expended chiefly upon churches and upon those psychic edifices which are begotten or influenced by churches. His "anti-world" has the medieval, thoroughly provincial, quintessentially Catholic atmosphere of an Erin trying desperately to enjoy its political independence. He worked at *Ulysses* in many foreign lands, and from all of them he looked back in faith and kinship upon Mother Church and Ireland. He used his foreign stopping-places merely as anchors to steady his ship in the maelstrom of his Irish reminiscences and resentments. Yet Ulysses does not strain back to his Ithaca—on the contrary, he makes frantic efforts to rid himself of his Irish heritage.

181 We might suppose this behaviour to be of only local interest and expect it to leave the rest of the world quite cold. But it does not leave the world cold. The local phenomenon seems to be more or less universal, to judge from its effects on Joyce's contemporaries. The cap must fit. There must exist a whole community of moderns who are so numerous that they have been able to devour ten editions of *Ulysses* since 1922. The book must mean something to them, must even reveal something that they did not know or feel before. They are not infernally bored by it, but are helped, refreshed, instructed, converted, "restratified." Obviously, they are thrown into a desirable state of some sort, for otherwise only the blackest hatred could enable the reader to go through the book from page 1 to page 735 with attention and without fatal attacks of drowsiness. I therefore surmise that medieval Catholic Ireland covers a geographical area of whose size I have hitherto been ignorant; it is certainly far larger than the

area indicated on the ordinary map. This Catholic Middle Ages, with its Messrs. Dedalus and Bloom, seems to be pretty well universal. There must be whole sections of the population that are so bound to their spiritual environment that nothing less than Joycean explosives are required to break through their hermetic isolation. I am convinced that this is so: we are still stuck in the Middle Ages up to the ears. And it is because Joyce's contemporaries are so riddled with medieval prejudices that such prophets of negation as he and Freud are needed to reveal to them the other side of reality.

Of course, this tremendous task could hardly be accomplished by a man who with Christian benevolence tried to make people turn an unwilling eye on the shadow-side of things. That would amount only to their looking on with perfect unconcern. No, the revelation must be brought about by the appropriate attitude of mind, and Joyce is again a master here. Only in this way can the forces of negative emotion be mobilized. *Ulysses* shows how one should execute Nietzsche's "sacrilegious backward grasp." Joyce sets about it coldly and objectively, and shows himself more "bereft of gods" than Nietzsche ever dreamed of being. All this on the implicit and correct assumption that the fascinating influence exerted by the spiritual environment has nothing to do with reason, but everything with feeling. One should not be misled into thinking that because Joyce reveals a world that is horribly bleak and bereft of gods, it is inconceivable that anyone should derive the slightest comfort from his book. Strange as it may sound, it remains true that the world of *Ulysses* is a better one than the world of those who are hopelessly bound to the darkness of their spiritual birthplaces. Even though the evil and destructive elements predominate, they are far more valuable than the "good" that has come down to us from the past and proves in reality to be a ruthless tyrant, an illusory system of prejudices that robs life of its richness, emasculates it, and enforces a moral compulsion which in the end is unendurable. Nietzsche's "slave-uprising in morals" would be a good motto for *Ulysses*. What frees the prisoner of a system is an "objective" recognition of his world and of his own nature. Just as the arch-Bolshevist revels in his unshaven appearance, so the man who is bound in spirit finds a rapturous joy in saying straight out for once exactly how things are in his world.

121

For the man who is dazzled by the light the darkness is a blessing, and the boundless desert is a paradise to the escaped prisoner. It is nothing less than redemption for the medieval man of today not to have to be the embodiment of goodness and beauty and common sense. Looked at from the shadow-side, ideals are not beacons on mountain peaks, but taskmasters and gaolers, a sort of metaphysical police originally thought up on Sinai by the tyrannical demagogue Moses and thereafter foisted upon mankind by a clever ruse.

183 From the causal point of view Joyce is a victim of Roman Catholic authoritarianism, but considered teleologically he is a reformer who for the present is satisfied with negation, a Protestant nourished by his own protests. Atrophy of feeling is a characteristic of modern man and always shows itself as a reaction when there is too much feeling around, and in particular too much false feeling. From the lack of feeling in *Ulysses* we may infer a hideous sentimentality in the age that produced it. But are we really so sentimental today?

184 Again a question which the future must answer. Still, there is a good deal of evidence to show that we actually are involved in a sentimentality hoax of gigantic proportions. Think of the lamentable role of popular sentiment in wartime! Think of our so-called humanitarianism! The psychiatrist knows only too well how each of us becomes the helpless but not pitiable victim of his own sentiments. Sentimentality is the superstructure erected upon brutality. Unfeelingness is the counter-position and inevitably suffers from the same defects. The success of *Ulysses* proves that even its lack of feeling has a positive effect on the reader, so that we must infer an excess of sentiment which he is quite willing to have damped down. I am deeply convinced that we are not only stuck in the Middle Ages but also are caught in our own sentimentality. It is therefore quite comprehensible that a prophet should arise to teach our culture a compensatory lack of feeling. Prophets are always disagreeable and usually have bad manners, but it is said that they occasionally hit the nail on the head. There are, as we know, major and minor prophets, and history will decide to which of them Joyce belongs. Like every true prophet, the artist is the unwitting mouthpiece of the psychic secrets of his time, and is often as unconscious as a sleep-walker. He supposes that it is he who

speaks, but the spirit of the age is his prompter, and whatever
this spirit says is proved true by its effects.

185   *Ulysses* is a *document humain* of our time and, what is more,
it harbours a secret. It can release the spiritually bound, and its
coldness can freeze all sentimentality—and even normal feeling
—to the marrow. But these salutary effects do not exhaust its
powers. The notion that the devil himself stood sponsor to the
work, if interesting, is hardly a satisfactory hypothesis. There is
life in it, and life is never exclusively evil and destructive. To be
sure, the side of it that is most tangible seems negative and dis-
ruptive; but one senses behind it something intangible—a secret
purpose which lends it meaning and value. Is this patchwork
quilt of words and images perhaps "symbolic"? I am not thinking of an allegory (heaven forbid!), but of the symbol as an
expression of something whose nature we cannot grasp. In that
case a hidden meaning would doubtless shine through the curious fabric at some point, here and there notes would resound
that had been heard at other times and places, maybe in unusual
dreams or in the cryptic wisdom of forgotten races. This possibility cannot be contested, but, for myself, I cannot find the key.
On the contrary, the book seems to me to be written in the full
light of consciousness; it is not a dream and not a revelation of
the unconscious. Compared with *Zarathustra* or the second part
of *Faust,* it shows an even stronger purposiveness and sense of
direction. This is probably why *Ulysses* does not bear the features of a symbolic work. Of course, one senses the archetypal
background. Behind Dedalus and Bloom there stand the eternal figures of spiritual and carnal man; Mrs. Bloom perhaps con-
ceals an anima entangled in worldliness, and Ulysses himself
might be the hero. But the book does not focus upon this background; it veers away in the opposite direction and strives to
attain the utmost objectivity of consciousness. It is obviously not
symbolic and has no intention of being so. Were it none the less
symbolic in certain parts, then the unconscious, in spite of every
precaution, would have played the author a trick or two. For
when something is "symbolic," it means that a person divines its
hidden, ungraspable nature and is trying desperately to capture
in words the secret that eludes him. Whether it is something of
the world he is striving to grasp or something of the spirit, he
must turn to it with all his mental powers and penetrate all its

iridescent veils in order to bring to the light of day the gold that lies jealously hidden in the depths.

186   But the shattering thing about *Ulysses* is that behind the thousand veils nothing lies hidden; it turns neither to the world nor to the spirit but, cold as the moon looking on from cosmic space,[14] leaves the comedy of genesis and decay to pursue its course. I sincerely hope that *Ulysses* is not symbolic, for if it were it would have failed in its purpose. What kind of anxiously guarded secret might it be that is hidden with matchless care under seven hundred and thirty-five unendurable pages? It is better not to waste one's time and energy on a fruitless treasure-hunt. Indeed, there *ought not* to be anything symbolic behind the book, for if there were our consciousness would be dragged back into world and spirit, perpetuating Messrs. Bloom and Dedalus to all eternity, befooled by the ten thousand facets of life. This is just what *Ulysses* seeks to prevent: it wants to be an eye of the moon, a consciousness detached from the object, in thrall neither to the gods nor to sensuality, and bound neither by love nor by hate, neither by conviction nor by prejudice. *Ulysses* does not preach this but practises it—detachment of consciousness[15] is the goal that shimmers through the fog of this book. This, surely, is its real secret, the secret of a new cosmic consciousness; and it is revealed not to him who has conscientiously waded through the seven hundred and thirty-five pages, but to him who has gazed at his world and his own mind for seven hundred and thirty-five days with the eyes of Ulysses. This space of time, at any rate, is to be taken symbolically—"a time, times and a half a time"—an indefinite time, therefore; but sufficiently long for the transformation to take place. The detachment of consciousness can be expressed in the Homeric image of Odysseus sailing the straits between Scylla and Charybdis, between the Symplegades, the clashing rocks of the world and the spirit; or, in the imagery of the Dublin inferno, between

14 Gilbert, p. 355 n.: ". . . to take, so to speak, a God's-eye view of the cosmos."
15 Gilbert likewise stresses this detachment. He says on p. 21: "The attitude of the author of *Ulysses* towards his personages is one of serene detachment." (I would put a question-mark after "serene.") P. 22: "All facts of any kind, mental or material, sublime or ridiculous, have an equivalence of meaning for the artist." P. 23: "In this detachment, as absolute as the indifference of Nature herself towards her children, we may see one of the causes of the apparent 'realism' of *Ulysses*."

Father John Conmee and the Viceroy of Ireland, "a light crumpled throwaway," drifting down the Liffey (p. 239):

Elijah, skiff, light crumpled throwaway, sailed eastward by flanks of ships and trawlers, amid an archipelago of corks, beyond new Wapping street past Benson's ferry, and by the threemasted schooner *Rosevean* from Bridgwater with bricks.

187   Can this detachment of consciousness, this depersonalization of the personality, can this be the Ithaca of the Joycean Odyssey?

188   One might suppose that in a world of nothing but nothingness at least the "I"—James Joyce himself—would be left over. But has anyone noticed the appearance, among all the unhappy, shadowy "I"s of this book, of a single, actual ego? True, every figure in *Ulysses* is superlatively real, none of them could be other than what they are, they are themselves in every respect. And yet not one of them has an ego, there is no acutely conscious, human centre, an island surrounded by warm heart's blood, so small and yet so vitally important. All the Dedaluses, Blooms, Harrys, Lynches, Mulligans, and the rest of them talk and go about as in a collective dream that begins nowhere and ends nowhere, that takes place only because "No-man"—an unseen Odysseus—dreams it. None of them knows this, and yet all live for the sole reason that a god bids them live. That is how life is—*vita somnium breve*—and that is why the Joycean figures are so real. But the ego that embraces them all appears nowhere. It betrays itself by nothing, by no judgment, no sympathy, not a single anthropomorphism. The ego of the creator of these figures is not to be found. It is as though it had dissolved into the countless figures of *Ulysses*.[16] And yet, or rather for that very reason, all and everything, even the missing punctuation of the final chapter, is Joyce himself. His detached, contemplative consciousness, dispassionately embracing in one glance the timeless simultaneity of the happenings of the sixteenth day of June, 1904, must say of all these appearances: *Tat tvam asi*, "That art thou"—"thou" in a higher sense, not the ego but the self. For the self alone embraces the ego and the non-ego, the infernal regions, the viscera, the *imagines et lares*, and the heavens.

16 As Joyce himself says in *A Portrait of the Artist as a Young Man* (1930 edn., p. 245): "The artist, like the God of Creation, remains within or behind or beyond or above his handiwork, invisible, refined out of existence, indifferent, paring his fingernails."

189   Whenever I read *Ulysses* there comes into my mind a Chinese picture, published by Richard Wilhelm,[17] of a yogi in meditation, with five human figures growing out of the top of his head and five more figures growing out of the top of each of *their* heads. This picture portrays the spiritual state of the yogi who is about to rid himself of his ego and to pass over into the more complete, more objective state of the self. This is the state of the "moon-disk, at rest and alone," of *sat-chit-ananda,* the epitome of being and not-being, the ultimate goal of the Eastern way of redemption, the priceless pearl of Indian and Chinese wisdom, sought and extolled through the centuries.

190   The "light crumpled throwaway" drifts towards the East. Three times this crumpled note turns up in *Ulysses,* each time mysteriously connected with Elijah. Twice we are told: "Elijah is coming." He actually does appear in the brothel scene (rightly compared by Middleton Murry to the Walpurgisnacht in *Faust*), where in Americanese he explains the secret of the note (p. 478):

> Boys, do it now. God's time is 12.25. Tell mother you'll be there. Rush your order and you play a slick ace. Join on right here! Book through to eternity junction, the nonstop run. Just one word more. Are you a god or a doggone clod? If the second advent came to Coney Island are we ready? Florry Christ, Stephen Christ, Zoe Christ, Bloom Christ, Kitty Christ, Lynch Christ, it's up to you to sense that cosmic force. Have we cold feet about the cosmos? No. Be on the side of the angels. Be a prism. *You have that something within, the higher self.*[18] You can rub shoulders with a Jesus, a Gautama, an Ingersoll. Are you all in this vibration? I say you are. You once nobble that, congregation, and a buck joyride to heaven becomes a back number. You got me? It's a lifebrightener, sure. The hottest stuff ever was. It's the whole pie with jam in. It's just the cutest snappiest line out. It is immense, supersumptuous. It restores.

191   One can see what has happened: the detachment of human consciousness and its consequent approximation to the divine—the whole basis and highest artistic achievement of *Ulysses*—suffers an infernal distortion in the drunken madhouse of the brothel as soon as it appears in the cloak of a traditional formula. Ulysses, the sorely tried wanderer, toils ever towards his

---

17 Wilhelm and Jung, *The Secret of the Golden Flower* (1962 edn.), p. 57. [The picture is reproduced in *Alchemical Studies*, p. 33.—EDITORS.]
18 My italics.

island home, back to his true self, beating his way through the turmoil of eighteen chapters, and, free at last from the fool's world of illusions, "looks on from afar," impassively. Thus he achieves what a Jesus or a Buddha achieved, and what Faust also strove for—the overcoming of a fool's world, liberation from the opposites. And just as Faust was dissolved in the Eternal Feminine, so it is Molly Bloom (whom Stuart Gilbert compares to the blossoming earth) who has the last word in her unpunctuated monologue, putting a blessed close to the hellish, shrieking dissonances with a harmonious final chord.

192   Ulysses is the creator-god in Joyce, a true demiurge who has freed himself from entanglement in the physical and mental world and contemplates them with detached consciousness. He is for Joyce what Faust was for Goethe, or Zarathustra for Nietzsche. He is the higher self who returns to his divine home after blind entanglement in *samsara*. In the whole book no Ulysses appears; the book itself is Ulysses, a microcosm of James Joyce, the world of the self and the self of the world in one. Ulysses can return home only when he has turned his back on the world of mind and matter. This is surely the message underlying that sixteenth day of June, 1904, the everyday of everyman, on which persons of no importance restlessly do and say things without beginning or aim—a shadowy picture, dreamlike, infernal, sardonic, negative, ugly, devilish, but true. A picture that could give one bad dreams or induce the mood of a cosmic Ash Wednesday, such as the Creator might have felt on August 1, 1914. After the optimism of the seventh day of creation the demiurge must have found it pretty difficult in 1914 to identify himself with his handiwork. *Ulysses* was written between 1914 and 1921—hardly the conditions for painting a particularly cheerful picture of the world or for taking it lovingly in one's arms (nor today either, for that matter). So it is not surprising that the demiurge in the artist sketched a negative picture, so blasphemously negative that in Anglo-Saxon countries the book was banned in order to avoid the scandal of its contradicting the creation story in Genesis! And that is how the misunderstood demiurge became Ulysses in search of his home.

193   There is so little feeling in *Ulysses* that it must be very pleasing to all aesthetes. But let us assume that the consciousness of *Ulysses* is not a moon but an ego that possesses judgment, under-

standing, and a feeling heart. Then the long road through the eighteen chapters would not only hold no delights but would be a road to Calvary; and the wanderer, overcome by so much suffering and folly, would sink down at nightfall into the arms of the Great Mother, who signifies the beginning and end of life. Under the cynicism of Ulysses there is hidden a great compassion; he knows the sufferings of a world that is neither beautiful nor good and, worse still, rolls on without hope through the eternally repeated everyday, dragging with it man's consciousness in an idiot dance through the hours, months, years. Ulysses has dared to take the step that leads to the detachment of consciousness from the object; he has freed himself from attachment, entanglement, and delusion, and can therefore turn homeward. He gives us more than a subjective expression of personal opinion, for the creative genius is never one but many, and he speaks in stillness to the souls of the multitude, whose meaning and destiny he embodies no less than the artist's own.

194   It seems to me now that all that is negative in Joyce's work, all that is cold-blooded, bizarre and banal, grotesque and devilish, is a positive virtue for which it deserves praise. Joyce's inexpressibly rich and myriad-faceted language unfolds itself in passages that creep along tapeworm fashion, terribly boring and monotonous, but the very boredom and monotony of it attain an epic grandeur that makes the book a *Mahabharata* of the world's futility and squalor. "From drains, clefts, cesspools, middens arise on all sides stagnant fumes" (p. 412). And in this open cloaca is reflected with blasphemous distortion practically everything that is highest in religious thought, exactly as in dreams. (Alfred Kubin's *Die andere Seite* is a country-cousin of the metropolitan *Ulysses*.)

195   Even this I willingly accept, for it cannot be denied. On the contrary, the transformation of eschatology into scatology proves the truth of Tertullian's dictum: *anima naturaliter christiana*. Ulysses shows himself a conscientious Antichrist and thereby proves that his Catholicism still holds together. He is not only a Christian but—still higher title to fame—a Buddhist, Shivaist, and a Gnostic (p. 481):

(*With a voice of waves.*) . . . White yoghin of the Gods. Occult pimander of Hermes Trismegistos. (*With a voice of whistling sea-*

wind.) Punarjanam patsypunjaub! I won't have my leg pulled. It has been said by one: beware of the left, the cult of Shakti. (*With a cry of stormbirds.*) Shakti, Shiva! Dark hidden Father! . . . Aum! Baum! Pyjaum! I am the light of the homestead, I am the dreamery creamery butter.

196   Is not that touching and significant? Even on the dunghill the oldest and noblest treasures of the spirit are not lost. There is no cranny in the psyche through which the divine afflatus could finally breathe out its life and perish in noisome filth. Old Hermes, father of all heretical bypaths, is right: "As above, so below." Stephen Dedalus, the bird-headed sky-man, trying to escape from the all too gaseous regions of the air, falls into an earthly slough and in the very depths encounters again the heights from which he fled. "And should I flee to the uttermost ends of the earth . . ." The close of this sentence is a blasphemy that furnishes the most convincing proof of this in all *Ulysses*.[19] Better still, that nosyparker Bloom, the perverse and impotent sensualist, experiences in the dirt something that had never happened to him before: his own transfiguration. Glad tidings: when the eternal signs have vanished from the heavens, the pig that hunts truffles finds them again in the earth. For they are indelibly stamped on the lowest as on the highest; only in the lukewarm intermediate realm that is accursed of God are they nowhere to be found.

197   Ulysses is absolutely objective and absolutely honest and therefore trustworthy. One can trust his testimony as to the

[19] [This passage has been difficult to interpret, for the quotation could not be located in *Ulysses*. Jung quoted the novel usually in English but here he uses German: "'Und flöh' ich ans äusserste Ende der Welt, so . . .' der Nachsatz ist des Ulysses beweiskräftige Blasphemie." This may be a reference to the beginning of a speech of Stephen Dedalus in the Circe episode (p. 476): "What went forth to the ends of the world to traverse not itself. God, the sun, Shakespeare, a commercial traveller, having itself traversed in reality itself, becomes that self. . . . Wait a second. Damn that fellow's noise in the street. . . ." The "noise in the street" is a gramophone playing a sacred cantata, *The Holy City*. Professor Ellmann has suggested a back-reference here to Stephen's remark to Deasy in the Nestor episode (ch. 2): "That is God. . . . A shout in the street." Jung could also have intended a Biblical allusion; cf. Psalm 139 : 7–9 (AV): ". . . whither shall I flee from thy presence? If I ascend up into heaven, thou art there: if I make my bed in hell, behold, thou art there. If I take the wings of the morning, and dwell in the uttermost parts of the sea . . ."—EDITORS.]

power and nugatoriness of the world and the spirit. Ulysses alone is reality, life, meaning; in him is comprised the whole phantasmagoria of mind and matter, of egos and non-egos. And here I would like to ask Mr. Joyce a question: "Have you noticed that you are a representation, a thought, perhaps a complex of Ulysses? That he stands about you like a hundred-eyed Argus, and has thought up for you a world and an anti-world, filling them with objects without which you could not be conscious of your ego at all?" I do not know what the worthy author would answer to this question. Nor is it any business of mine—there is nothing to stop me from indulging in metaphysics on my own. But one is driven to ask it when one sees how neatly the microcosm of Dublin, on that sixteenth day of June, 1904, has been fished out of the chaotic macrocosm of world history, how it is dissected and spread out on a glass slide in all its tasty details, and described with the most pedantic exactitude by a completely detached observer. Here are the streets, here are the houses and a young coupl·' out for a walk, a real Mr. Bloom goes about his advertising business, a real Stephen Dedalus diverts himself with aphoristic philosophy. It would be quite possible for Mr. Joyce himself to loom up at some Dublin street-corner. Why not? He is surely as real as Mr. Bloom and could therefore equally well be fished out, dissected, and described (as, for instance, in *A Portrait of the Artist as a Young Man*).

198   Who, then, is Ulysses? Doubtless he is a symbol of what makes up the totality, the oneness, of all the single appearances in *Ulysses* as a whole—Mr. Bloom, Stephen, Mrs. Bloom, and the rest, including Mr. Joyce. Try to imagine a being who is not a mere colourless conglomerate soul composed of an indefinite number of ill-assorted and antagonistic individual souls, but consists also of houses, street-processions, churches, the Liffey, several brothels, and a crumpled note on its way to the sea—and yet possesses a perceiving and registering consciousness! Such a monstrosity drives one to speculation, especially as one can prove nothing anyway and has to fall back on conjecture. I must confess that I suspect Ulysses of being a more comprehensive self who is the subject of all the objects on the glass slide, a being who acts as if he were Mr. Bloom or a printing-shop or a crumpled note, but actually is the "dark hidden Father" of his specimens. "I am the sacrificer and the sacrificed." In the lan-

guage of the infernal regions: "I am the dreamery creamery butter." When he turns to the world with a loving embrace, all the gardens blossom. But when he turns his back upon it, the empty everyday rolls on—*labitur et labetur in omne volubilis aevum.*[20]

199   The demiurge first created a world that in his vainglory seemed to him perfect; but looking upward he beheld a light which he had not created. Thereupon he turned back towards the place where was his home. But as he did so, his masculine creative power turned into feminine acquiescence, and he had to confess:

> All things ephemeral
> Are but a reflection;
> The unattainable
> Here finds perfection;
> The indescribable
> Here it is done;
> The Eternal Feminine
> Still draws us on.

200   From the specimen-slide far below upon earth, in Ireland, Dublin, 7 Eccles Street, from her bed as she grows sleepy at about two o'clock in the morning of the seventeenth of June, 1904, the voice of easy-going Mrs. Bloom speaks:

O and the sea the sea crimson sometimes like fire and the glorious sunsets and the figtrees in the Alameda gardens yes and all the queer little streets and pink and blue and yellow houses and the rosegardens and the jessamine and geraniums and cactuses and Gibraltar as a girl where I was a Flower of the mountain yes when I put the rose in my hair like the Andalusian girls used or shall I wear a red yes and how he kissed me under the Moorish wall and I thought well as well him as another and then I asked him with my eyes to ask again yes and then he asked me would I yes to say yes my mountain flower and first I put my arms around him yes and drew him down to me so he could feel my breasts all perfume yes and his heart was going like mad and yes I said yes I will Yes.

201   O *Ulysses,* you are truly a devotional book for the object-besotted, object-ridden white man! You are a spiritual exercise, an ascetic discipline, an agonizing ritual, an arcane procedure,

[20] [Horace, *Epistles,* 1.2.33 (trans. Fairclough: "yet on [the river] glides, and on it will glide, rolling its flood forever").—EDITORS.]

131

eighteen alchemical alembics piled on top of one another, where amid acids, poisonous fumes, and fire and ice, the homunculus of a new, universal consciousness is distilled!

202   You say nothing and betray nothing, O *Ulysses*, but you give us the works! Penelope need no longer weave her never-ending garment; she now takes her ease in the gardens of the earth, for her husband is home again, all his wanderings over. A world has passed away, and is made new.

203   Concluding remark: I am now getting on pretty well with my reading of *Ulysses*—forward!

APPENDIX

[The genesis of the foregoing paper is of interest, in that conflicting explanations have been published. The version that is believed to be authentic is given first:

(1) In par. 171, Jung stated that he wrote the article because a publisher asked him "what I thought about [Joyce], or rather about *Ulysses*." This was Dr. Daniel Brody, formerly head of Rhein-Verlag (Zurich), which published a German translation of *Ulysses* in 1927 (2nd and 3rd edns., 1930). Dr. Brody has recounted that, in 1930, he attended a lecture by Jung in Munich on "the psychology of the author." (This was probably an earlier version of the preceding paper, "Psychology and Literature.") Speaking with Jung later, Dr. Brody said that he felt Jung was referring to Joyce, without mentioning his name. Jung denied this but said that he was indeed interested in Joyce and had read part of *Ulysses*. Dr. Brody responded that the Rhein-Verlag was preparing to publish a literary review, and he would welcome an article on Joyce by Jung for the first issue. Jung agreed, and about a month later he delivered the article to Dr. Brody, who discovered that Jung had dealt with Joyce and *Ulysses* mainly from a clinical point of view and, so it seemed, harshly. He sent the article to Joyce, who cabled him, "Niedrigerhängen," meaning "Hang it lower" or, figuratively, "Show it up by printing it." (Joyce was quoting Frederick the Great, who upon seeing a placard attacking him directed that it be hung lower for all to behold.) Friends of Joyce, including Stuart Gilbert, advised Brody not to publish the article, though Jung at first insisted on its publication. In the meantime, political tensions had developed in Germany, so that the Rhein-Verlag decided to abandon the projected literary review,

and Dr. Brody therefore returned the article to Jung. Later, Jung revised the essay (modifying its severity) and published it in 1932 in the *Europäische Revue*. The original version has never come to light.

The foregoing summary is based partially on recent communications from Dr. Brody to the Editors and partially on the contents of a letter from Professor Richard Ellmann, who obtained a similar account from Dr. Brody. Professor Ellmann has stated that he will deal with the subject in a new edition of his biography of Joyce.

(2) In the first edition of his *James Joyce* (1959; p. 641), Professor Ellmann wrote that Brody asked Jung for a preface to the third edition (late 1930) of the German translation of *Ulysses*. Patricia Hutchins, in *James Joyce's World* (1957; p. 182), quotes Jung in an interview: "In the thirties I was asked to write an introduction to the German edition of *Ulysses,* but as such it was not a success. Later I published it in one of my books. My interest was not literary but professional. . . . The book was a most valuable document from my point of view. . . ."

(3) In a letter to Harriet Shaw Weaver, Sept. 27, 1930, from Paris, Joyce wrote: "The Rheinverlag wrote to Jung for a preface to the German edition of Gilbert's book. He replied with a very long and hostile attack . . . which they are much upset about, but I want them to use it. . . ." (*Letters,* ed. Stuart Gilbert, p. 294). Rhein-Verlag published a German edition of *James Joyce's "Ulysses": A Study,* as *Das Rätsel Ulysses,* in 1932. Mr. Gilbert stated, in a letter to the Editors: "I fear my memories of Jung's *Ulysses* essay remain vague, but . . . I feel fairly sure that Jung was asked to write the piece for my *Rätsel* and not for any German edition of *Ulysses."* Professor Ellmann has subsequently commented, in a letter: "I suspect that at some point in the negotiations with Jung the possibility of using the article also as a preface to Gilbert's book may well have arisen, either at Brody's suggestion or at Joyce's."

*

Jung sent Joyce a copy of the revised version of his essay, with the following letter (cf. Ellmann, *James Joyce,* p. 642):

Küsnacht-Zürich
Seestrasse 228
September 27th, 1932.

James Joyce Esq.
  Hotel Elite,
    Zürich
Dear Sir,

Your Ulysses has presented the world such an upsetting psychological problem that repeatedly I have been called in as a supposed authority on psychological matters.

Ulysses proved to be an exceedingly hard nut and it has forced my mind not only to most unusual efforts, but also to rather extravagant peregrinations (speaking from the standpoint of a scientist). Your book as a whole has given me no end of trouble and I was brooding over it for about three years until I succeeded to put myself into it. But I must tell you that I'm profoundly grateful to yourself as well as to your gigantic opus, because I learned a great deal from it. I shall probably never be quite sure whether I did enjoy it, because it meant too much grinding of nerves and of grey matter. I also don't know whether you will enjoy what I have written about Ulysses because I couldn't help telling the world how much I was bored, how I grumbled, how I cursed and how I admired. The 40 pages of non stop run in the end is a string of veritable psychological peaches. I suppose the devil's grandmother knows so much about the real psychology of a woman, I didn't.

Well I just try to recommend my little essay to you, as an amusing attempt of a perfect stranger who went astray in the labyrinth of your Ulysses and happened to get out of it again by sheer good luck. At all events you may gather from my article what Ulysses has done to a supposedly balanced psychologist.

With the expression of my deepest appreciation, I remain, dear Sir,

Yours faithfully
C. G. Jung

Jung's copy of *Ulysses* (cf. above, p. 109, n. 1) contains on its flyleaf the following inscription in Joyce's hand: "To Dr C. G. Jung, with grateful appreciation of his aid and counsel. James Joyce. Xmas 1934, Zurich." The copy is evidently the one that Jung owned when he wrote the essay, as some of the passages quoted therein have been marked in pencil.

—EDITORS.]

PICASSO [1]

204   As a psychiatrist, I almost feel like apologizing to the reader
for becoming involved in the excitement over Picasso. Had it
not been suggested to me from an authoritative quarter, I
should probably never have taken up my pen on the subject. It
is not that this painter and his strange art seem to me too slight a
theme—I have, after all, seriously concerned myself with his literary brother, James Joyce.[2] On the contrary, his problem has
my undivided interest, only it appears too wide, too difficult,
and too involved for me to hope that I could come anywhere
near to covering it fully in a short article. If I venture to voice
an opinion on the subject at all, it is with the express reservation
that I have nothing to say on the question of Picasso's "art" but
only on its psychology. I shall therefore leave the aesthetic problem to the art critics, and shall restrict myself to the psychology
underlying this kind of artistic creativeness.

205   For almost twenty years, I have occupied myself with the
psychology of the pictorial representation of psychic processes,
and I am therefore in a position to look at Picasso's pictures
from a professional point of view. On the basis of my experience, I can assure the reader that Picasso's psychic problems, so
far as they find expression in his work, are strictly analogous to
those of my patients. Unfortunately, I cannot offer proof on this
point, as the comparative material is known only to a few

---

1 [First published in the *Neue Zürcher Zeitung*, CLIII : 2 (Nov. 13, 1932); reprinted in *Wirklichkeit der Seele* (Zurich, 1934). Previously translated by Alda F.
Oertly for the *Papers of the Analytical Psychology Club of New York City* (1940);
another translation, by Ivo Jarosy, appeared in *Nimbus* (London), II : 2 (autumn,
1953). Both versions have been consulted in the present translation.

[The Kunsthaus, Zurich, held an exhibition of 460 works by Picasso from
Sept. 11 to Oct. 30, 1932.—EDITORS.]
2 " 'Ulysses': A Monologue," supra.

specialists. My further observations will therefore appear unsupported, and require the reader's good will and imagination.

206   Non-objective art draws its contents essentially from "inside." This "inside" cannot correspond to consciousness, since consciousness contains images of objects as they are generally seen, and whose appearance must therefore necessarily conform to general expectations. Picasso's object, however, appears different from what is generally expected—so different that it no longer seems to refer to any object of outer experience at all. Taken chronologically, his works show a growing tendency to withdraw from the empirical objects, and an increase in those elements which do not correspond to any outer experience but come from an "inside" situated behind consciousness—or at least behind that consciousness which, like a universal organ of perception set over and above the five senses, is orientated towards the outer world. Behind consciousness there lies not the absolute void but the unconscious psyche, which affects consciousness from behind and from inside, just as much as the outer world affects it from in front and from outside. Hence those pictorial elements which do not correspond to any "outside" must originate from "inside."

207   As this "inside" is invisible and cannot be imagined, even though it can affect consciousness in the most pronounced manner, I induce those of my patients who suffer mainly from the effects of this "inside" to set them down in pictorial form as best they can. The aim of this method of expression is to make the unconscious contents accessible and so bring them closer to the patient's understanding. The therapeutic effect of this is to prevent a dangerous splitting-off of the unconscious processes from consciousness. In contrast to objective or "conscious" representations, all pictorial representations of processes and effects in the psychic background are *symbolic*. They point, in a rough and approximate way, to a meaning that for the time being is unknown. It is, accordingly, altogether impossible to determine anything with any degree of certainty in a single, isolated instance. One only has the feeling of strangeness and of a confusing, incomprehensible jumble. One does not know what is actually meant or what is being represented. The possibility of understanding comes only from a comparative study of many such pictures. Because of their lack of artistic imagination, the

pictures of patients are generally clearer and simpler, and therefore easier to understand, than those of modern artists.

208   Among patients, two groups may be distinguished: the *neurotics* and the *schizophrenics*. The first group produces pictures of a synthetic character, with a pervasive and unified feeling-tone. When they are completely abstract, and therefore lacking the element of feeling, they are at least definitely symmetrical or convey an unmistakable meaning. The second group, on the other hand, produces pictures which immediately reveal their alienation from feeling. At any rate they communicate no unified, harmonious feeling-tone but, rather, contradictory feelings or even a complete lack of feeling. From a purely formal point of view, the main characteristic is one of fragmentation, which expresses itself in the so-called "lines of fracture"—that is, a series of psychic "faults" (in the geological sense) which run right through the picture. The picture leaves one cold, or disturbs one by its paradoxical, unfeeling, and grotesque unconcern for the beholder. This is the group to which Picasso belongs.[3]

209   In spite of the obvious differences between the two groups, their productions have one thing in common: their *symbolic content*. In both cases the meaning is an implied one, but the neurotic searches for the meaning and for the feeling that corresponds to it, and takes pains to communicate it to the beholder. The schizophrenic hardly ever shows any such inclination; rather, it seems as though he were the victim of this meaning. It is as though he had been overwhelmed and swallowed up by it, and had been dissolved into all those elements which the neu-

---

[3] By this I do not mean that anyone who belongs to these two groups suffers from either neurosis or schizophrenia. Such a classification merely means that in the one case a psychic disturbance will probably result in ordinary neurotic symptoms, while in the other it will produce schizoid symptoms. In the case under discussion, the designation "schizophrenic" does not, therefore, signify a diagnosis of the mental illness schizophrenia, but merely refers to a disposition or habitus on the basis of which a serious psychological disturbance could produce schizophrenia. Hence I regard neither Picasso nor Joyce as psychotics, but count them among a large number of people whose habitus it is to react to a profound psychic disturbance not with an ordinary psychoneurosis but with a schizoid syndrome. As the above statement has given rise to some misunderstanding, I have considered it necessary to add this psychiatric explanation. [Jung's article in the *Zeitung* was followed by replies in the press, provoked especially by the observation on schizophrenia in par. 208. Consequently, Jung added this note in the 1934 version.—EDITORS.]

rotic at least tries to master. What I said about Joyce holds good for schizophrenic forms of expression too: nothing comes to meet the beholder, everything turns away from him; even an occasional touch of beauty seems only like an inexcusable delay in withdrawal. It is the ugly, the sick, the grotesque, the incomprehensible, the banal that are sought out—not for the purpose of expressing anything, but only in order to obscure; an obscurity, however, which has nothing to conceal, but spreads like a cold fog over desolate moors; the whole thing quite pointless, like a spectacle that can do without a spectator.

210   With the first group, one can divine what they are trying to express; with the second, what they are unable to express. In both cases, the content is full of secret meaning. A series of images of either kind, whether in drawn or written form, begins as a rule with the symbol of the Nekyia—the journey to Hades, the descent into the unconscious, and the leave-taking from the upper world. What happens afterwards, though it may still be expressed in the forms and figures of the day-world, gives intimations of a hidden meaning and is therefore symbolic in character. Thus Picasso starts with the still objective pictures of the Blue Period—the blue of night, of moonlight and water, the Tuat-blue of the Egyptian underworld. He dies, and his soul rides on horseback into the beyond. The day-life clings to him, and a woman with a child steps up to him warningly. As the day is woman to him, so is the night; psychologically speaking, they are the light and the dark soul (anima). The dark one sits waiting, expecting him in the blue twilight, and stirring up morbid presentiments. With the change of colour, we enter the underworld. The world of objects is death-struck, as the horrifying masterpiece of the syphilitic, tubercular, adolescent prostitute makes plain. The motif of the prostitute begins with the entry into the beyond, where he, as a departed soul, encounters a number of others of his kind. When I say "he," I mean that personality in Picasso which suffers the underworld fate—the man in him who does not turn towards the day-world, but is fatefully drawn into the dark; who follows not the accepted ideals of goodness and beauty, but the demoniacal attraction of ugliness and evil. It is these antichristian and Luciferian forces that well up in modern man and engender an all-pervading sense of doom, veiling the bright world of day with the mists of Hades,

138

infecting it with deadly decay, and finally, like an earthquake, dissolving it into fragments, fractures, discarded remnants, debris, shreds, and disorganized units. Picasso and his exhibition are a sign of the times, just as much as the twenty-eight thousand people who came to look at his pictures.

211   When such a fate befalls a man who belongs to the neurotic group, he usually encounters the unconscious in the form of the "Dark One," a Kundry of horribly grotesque, primeval ugliness or else of infernal beauty. In Faust's metamorphosis, Gretchen, Helen, Mary, and the abstract "Eternal Feminine" correspond to the four female figures of the Gnostic underworld, Eve, Helen, Mary, and Sophia. And just as Faust is embroiled in murderous happenings and reappears in changed form, so Picasso changes shape and reappears in the underworld form of the tragic Harlequin—a motif that runs through numerous paintings. It may be remarked in passing that Harlequin is an ancient chthonic god.[4]

212   The descent into ancient times has been associated ever since Homer's day with the Nekyia. Faust turns back to the crazy primitive world of the witches' sabbath and to a chimerical vision of classical antiquity. Picasso conjures up crude, earthy shapes, grotesque and primitive, and resurrects the soullessness of ancient Pompeii in a cold, glittering light—even Giulio Romano could not have done worse! Seldom or never have I had a patient who did not go back to neolithic art forms or revel in evocations of Dionysian orgies. Harlequin wanders like Faust through all these forms, though sometimes nothing betrays his presence but his wine, his lute, or the bright lozenges of his jester's costume. And what does he learn on his wild journey through man's millennial history? What quintessence will he distil from this accumulation of rubbish and decay, from these half-born or aborted possibilities of form and colour? What symbol will appear as the final cause and meaning of all this disintegration?

213   In view of the dazzling versatility of Picasso, one hardly dares to hazard a guess, so for the present I would rather speak of what I have found in my patients' material. The Nekyia is no aimless and purely destructive fall into the abyss, but a meaningful *katabasis eis antron*, a descent into the cave of initiation and secret

4 I am indebted to Dr. W. Kaegi for this information.

knowledge. The journey through the psychic history of mankind has as its object the restoration of the whole man, by awakening the memories in the blood. The descent to the Mothers enabled Faust to raise up the sinfully whole human being—Paris united with Helen—that *homo totus* who was forgotten when contemporary man lost himself in one-sidedness. It is he who at all times of upheaval has caused the tremor of the upper world, and always will. This man stands opposed to the man of the present, because he is the one who ever is as he was, whereas the other is what he is only for the moment. With my patients, accordingly, the *katabasis* and *katalysis* are followed by a recognition of the bipolarity of human nature and of the necessity of conflicting pairs of opposites. After the symbols of madness experienced during the period of disintegration there follow images which represent the coming together of the opposites: light/dark, above/below, white/black, male/female, etc. In Picasso's latest paintings, the motif of the union of opposites is seen very clearly in their direct juxtaposition. One painting (although traversed by numerous lines of fracture) even contains the conjunction of the light and dark anima. The strident, uncompromising, even brutal colours of the latest period reflect the tendency of the unconscious to master the conflict by violence (colour = feeling).

214   This state of things in the psychic development of a patient is neither the end nor the goal. It represents only a broadening of his outlook, which now embraces the whole of man's moral, bestial, and spiritual nature without as yet shaping it into a living unity. Picasso's *drame intérieur* has developed up to this last point before the dénouement. As to the future Picasso, I would rather not try my hand at prophecy, for this inner adventure is a hazardous affair and can lead at any moment to a standstill or to a catastrophic bursting asunder of the conjoined opposites. Harlequin is a tragically ambiguous figure, even though—as the initiated may discern—he already bears on his costume the symbols of the next stage of development. He is indeed the hero who must pass through the perils of Hades, but will he succeed? That is a question I cannot answer. Harlequin gives me the creeps—he is too reminiscent of that "motley fellow, like a buffoon" in *Zarathustra*, who jumped over the unsuspecting rope-dancer (another Pagliacci) and thereby brought about his death. Zarathus-

tra then spoke the words that were to prove so horrifyingly true of Nietzsche himself: "Your soul will be dead even sooner than your body: fear nothing more!" Who the buffoon is, is made plain as he cries out to the rope-dancer, his weaker *alter ego:* "To one better than yourself you bar the way!" He is the greater personality who bursts the shell, and this shell is sometimes—the brain.

BIBLIOGRAPHY

BIBLIOGRAPHY

AGRIPPA VON NETTESHEIM, HEINRICH CORNELIUS. *De incertitudine et vanitate scientiarum et artium.* Strasbourg, 1622. (Original edn., Cologne, 1527.)

AUGUSTINE, SAINT. *Confessions.* Translated by Francis Joseph Sheed. London and New York, 1951.

BARLACH, ERNST. *Der tote Tag.* Berlin, 1912. 2nd edn., 1918.

BENOÎT, PIERRE. *Atlantida.* Translated by Mary C. Tongue and Mary Ross. New York, 1920. (Original: *L'Atlantide.* Paris, 1920.)

BERTHELOT, MARCELLIN. *Collection des anciens alchimistes grecs.* Paris, 1887–88. 3 vols. [Cited as "*Alch. grecs.*"]

BLAKE, WILLIAM. *The Complete Writings.* Edited by Geoffrey Keynes. London and New York, 1957.

BURCKHARDT, JACOB. *Letters.* Selected, edited, and translated by Alexander Dru. London and New York, 1955.

CARUS, KARL GUSTAV. *Psyche.* Edited by Ludwig Klages. Jena, 1926. (Original edn., Pforzheim, 1846.)

COLONNA, FRANCESCO. *Hypnerotomachia Poliphili.* Venice, 1499.

———. See also FIERZ-DAVID.

CURTIUS, ERNEST ROBERT. *James Joyce und sein Ulysses.* Zurich, 1929.

EBERS, GEORG (ed.). *Papyros Ebers. Das hermetische Buch über die Arzneimittel der alten Aegypter.* Leipzig, 1875. 2 vols.

ECKERMANN, JOHANN PETER. *Conversations with Goethe.* Translated by R. O. Moon. London [1951].

ELLMANN, RICHARD. *James Joyce.* New York and London, 1959.

ERMATINGER, EMIL (ed.). *Philosophie der Litteraturwissenschaft.* Berlin, 1930.

[FIERZ-DAVID, LINDA.] *The Dream of Poliphilo.* Related and interpreted by Linda Fierz-David. Translated by Mary Hottinger. New York (Bollingen Series), 1950.

FREUD, SIGMUND. *The Standard Edition of the Complete Psychological Works*. Translated under the General Editorship of James Strachey. London, 1953– . 24 vols.

——. "Delusions and Dreams in Jensen's *Gradiva*." Translated by James Strachey. (Standard Edition, vol. 9, pp. 7–95.) (Orig. 1907.)

——. *The Future of an Illusion*. Translated by W. D. Robson-Scott. (Standard Edition, vol. 21, pp. 5–56.) (Orig. 1927.)

——. *The Interpretation of Dreams*. Translated by James Strachey. (Standard Edition, vols. 4, 5.) (Orig. 1900.)

——. *Jokes and their Relation to the Unconscious*. Translated by James Strachey. (Standard Edition, vol. 8.) (Orig. 1905.)

——. *Leonardo da Vinci and a Memory of His Childhood*. Translated by Alan Tyson. (Standard Edition, vol. 11, pp. 63–137.) (Orig. 1910.)

——. *Moses and Monotheism*. Translated by James Strachey. (Standard Edition, vol. 23, pp. 7–137.) (Orig. 1939.)

——. *The Psychopathology of Everyday Life*. Translated by Alan Tyson. (Standard Edition, vol. 6.) (Orig. 1901.)

——. *Totem and Taboo*. Translated by James Strachey. (Standard Edition, vol. 13, pp. 1–161.) (Orig. 1912.)

GESSNER, CONRAD. *Epistolarum medicinalium . . . libri III*. Zurich, 1577.

GIEDION-WELCKER, CAROLA. "Ein sprachliches Experiment von James Joyce," *Neue Schweizer Rundschau* (Zurich), Sept. 1929, pp. 660–77.

GILBERT, STUART. *James Joyce's "Ulysses": A Study*. New York and London, 1930.

——. See also JOYCE, *Letters*.

GOETHE, JOHANN WOLFGANG VON. *Faust, Part Two*. Translated by Philip Wayne. (Penguin Classics.) Harmondsworth and Baltimore, 1959.

GOETZ, BRUNO. *Das Reich ohne Raum*. Potsdam, 1919. 2nd edn., enlarged, Constance, 1925.

GUTMANN, BRUNO. *Die Stammeslehren der Dschagga*. (Arbeiten zur Entwicklungspsychologie, 12, 16, 19.) Munich, 1932–38. 3 vols.

HAGGARD, HENRY RIDER. *She*. London, 1887.

——. *Ayesha: The Return of She*. London, 1905.

HALL, G. STANLEY. *Life and Confessions of a Psychologist*. New York and London, 1923.

HERMAS. *The Shepherd*. In: *The Apostolic Fathers*. With an English translation by Kirsopp Lake. London and New York (Loeb Classical Library), 1912–13. 2 vols. (Vol. 2, pp. 6–305.)

[HERMES TRISMEGISTUS.] *Poimandres*. In: WALTER SCOTT (ed. and trans.). *Hermetica*. Oxford, 1924–36. 4 vols. (Vol. 1, pp. 114–133.)

HOFFMANN, ERNST THEODOR WILHELM (Amadeus). *Der goldene Topf*. Edited by W. F. Mainland. Oxford, 1942. English version: "The Golden Pot." In: J. M. COHEN (ed.). *Tales from Hoffmann*. Translated by various hands (in this instance, Thomas Carlyle). London, 1951. (Pp. 19–108.)

HORACE. *Satires, Epistles and Ars poetica*. With an English translation by H. R. Fairclough. London and New York (Loeb Classical Library), 1926.

HUTCHINS, PATRICIA. *James Joyce's World*. London, 1957.

[*I Ching*.] *The Yi King*. Translated by James Legge. (Sacred Books of the East, 16: Sacred Books of China: The Texts of Confucianism, Part Two.) Oxford, 1882.

——. *I Ging (Dschou I)*. *Das Buch der Wandlungen*. Translated into German by Richard Wilhelm. Jena, 1924.

——. *The I Ching, or Book of Changes*. The [foregoing] Richard Wilhelm translation, rendered into English by Cary F. Baynes. With a foreword by C. G. Jung. New York (Bollingen Series), 1950; London, 1951. 2 vols. 3rd edn. in 1 vol., 1967.

JAFFÉ, ANIELA. "Bilder und Symbole aus E. T. A. Hoffmanns Märchen Der Goldene Topf." In: C. G. JUNG. *Gestaltungen des Unbewussten*. Zurich, 1950.

JANET, PIERRE. *Névroses et idées fixes*. Paris, 1898. 2 vols.

JENSEN, WILHELM. *Gradiva: ein pompejanisches Phantasiestück*. Dresden and Leipzig, 1903.

JOYCE, JAMES. *Finnegans Wake*. London and New York, 1939.

——. *Letters*. Edited by Stuart Gilbert. New York and London, 1957.

——. *A Portrait of the Artist as a Young Man*. (Travellers' Library.) London, 1930. (Original edn., 1916.)

——. *Ulysses*. Paris, 10th printing, 1928.

——. *Work in Progress*. Serially in: *transition* (Paris), 1 (May 1927)–18 (Nov. 1929).

JUNG, CARL GUSTAV. *Civilization in Transition. Collected Works,** vol. 10.

——. "Concerning Rebirth." In: *Collected Works,* vol. 9, part i.

——. "Foreword to the *I Ching*." In: *Collected Works,* vol. 11.

——. "Instinct and the Unconscious." In: *Collected Works,* vol. 8.

——. *Memories, Dreams, Reflections*. Recorded and edited by Aniela Jaffé. Translated by Richard and Clara Winston. New York and London (separate editions, differently paginated), 1963.

——. "On the Nature of the Psyche." In: *Collected Works,* vol. 8.

——. "Paracelsus as a Spiritual Phenomenon." In: *Collected Works,* vol. 13.

——. *The Practice of Psychotherapy. Collected Works,* vol. 16.

——. *Psychological Types. Collected Works,* vol. 6. Alternative version: *Psychological Types*. Translated by H. G. Baynes. London and New York, 1923.

——. *Psychology and Alchemy. Collected Works,* vol. 12.

——. "A Study in the Process of Individuation." In: *Collected Works,* vol. 9, part i.

——. *Symbols of Transformation. Collected Works,* vol. 5.

——. "The Transcendent Function." In: *Collected Works,* vol. 8.

——. "Wotan." In: *Collected Works,* vol. 10.

KERÉNYI, C. *Asklepios: Archetypal Image of the Physician's Existence*. Translated by Ralph Manheim. New York (Bollingen Series), 1959; London, 1961. (Original: *Der göttliche Arzt*.)

KLAGES, LUDWIG. *Der Geist als Widersacher der Seele*. Leipzig, 1929–32. 3 vols.

KUBIN, ALFRED. *Die andere Seite*. Munich, 1909.

"Liber quartorum." See "Platonis . . ."

MELVILLE, HERMAN. *Moby Dick; or, The Whale*. New York, 1851.

MEYRINK, GUSTAV. *Das grüne Gesicht*. Leipzig, 1916.

---

* For details of the *Collected Works of C. G. Jung,* see announcement at end of this volume.

MYLIUS, JOHANN DANIEL. *Philosophia reformata.* Frankfurt a. M., 1622.

NIETZSCHE, FRIEDRICH WILHELM. *Ecce Homo* [*and Poems*]. Translated by Anthony M. Ludovici. (Complete Works, 17.) Edinburgh, London, and New York, 1911.

——. *Thus Spake Zarathustra.* Translated by Thomas Common. (Complete Works, 11.) London and New York, 1909.

PARACELSUS (Aureolus Philippus Theophrastus Bombast von Hohenheim). *Opera, Bücher und Schrifften* . . . durch Joannem Huserum in Truck gegeben. Strasbourg, 1589-91. 10 parts. Reprinted 1603, 1616. 2 vols. [Cited as "Huser" or *"Opera."*]

——. *Sämtliche Werke.* Translated (from the 1589–91 Huser edition) into modern German by Bernhard Aschner. Jena, 1926–32. 4 vols.

——. *Selected Writings.* Edited with an introduction by Jolande Jacobi. Translated by Norbert Guterman. New York (Bollingen Series) and London, 1951; 2nd edn., 1958.

——. *Archidoxis magicae.* In: *Opera* (see above), vol. II, 544–73.

——. *Das Buch Paragranum.* Edited by Franz Strunz. Jena, 1903.

——. *De caducis.* In: *Opera,* vol. I, 589–607.

——. *De morbis amentium.* In: *Opera,* vol. I, 486–506.

——. *De transmutationibus rerum naturalium.* In: *Opera,* vol. I, 898–902.

——. *De vita longa.* Edited by Adam von Bodenstein. Basel, 1562.

——. *Fragmenta medica.* Liber IV Columnarum. In: *Opera,* vol. I, 131–67.

——. *Fragmenta ad Paramirum.* In: *Opera,* vol. I, 132.

——. *Labyrinthus medicorum errantium.* In: *Opera,* vol. I, 264–82.

——. *Liber Azoth.* In: *Opera,* vol. II, 519–43.

——. *Von dem Podagra.* In: *Opera,* vol. I, 539–42.

"Platonis Liber quartorum." In: *Theatrum chemicum.* Ursel and Strasbourg, 1602–61. 6 vols. (Vol. 5, pp. 114–208.)

Poimandres. See HERMES TRISMEGISTUS.

SCHILLER, JOHANN CHRISTOPH FRIEDRICH. "On Naïve and Sentimental Poetry." In: *Essays Aesthetical and Philosophical.* London, 1875. (Pp. 262–332.)

SLOCUM, JOHN J., and HERBERT CAHOON. *A Bibliography of James Joyce.* New Haven, 1953.

SPITTELER, CARL. *Olympischer Frühling.* Jena, 1922. 2 vols.

——. *Prometheus and Epimetheus.* Translated by James Fullarton Muirhead. London, 1931.

Theatrum chemicum. See "Platonis. . . ."

WILHELM, HELLMUT. "The Concept of Time in the Book of Changes." In: *Man and Time.* (Papers from the Eranos Yearbooks, 3.) New York (Bollingen Series) and London, 1957.

WILHELM, RICHARD (trans.). *The Secret of the Golden Flower.* With a foreword and commentary by C. G. Jung. Translated by Cary F. Baynes. New York and London, 1931; 2nd edn., 1962.

——. See also *I Ching; I Ging.*

INDEX

INDEX

ARK PAPERBACKS

THE AWAKENING EARTH

This impressive, stimulating tour de force is an exciting challenge to our traditional view of ourselves and our place in the universe. Peter Russell puts forward the idea of the earth as a collective self-regulating living organism, and invites us to join in an exploration of humanity's potential as seen through the eyes of the planet. Through this we share with the author an inner vision of our evolutionary future. Drawing on the work of physicists, psychologists, philosophers and mystics, Peter Russell shows that human society may be about to make a quantum leap in evolution as significant as the emergence of life itself some three and a half million years ago.

PETER RUSSELL

Peter Russell was an honorary scholar at Gonville and Caius College, Cambridge, where he studied mathematics, theoretical physics, experimental psychology and later computer science. He has undertaken research on the psychology of meditation and has appeared frequently on radio and television. Amongst his publications are *The TM Technique* and *The Brain Book*. In addition to teaching meditation, Peter Russell lectures frequently in Europe and the United States, and acts as a major consultant on the development of learning processes to several major international companies.

ISBN 0-7448-0012-9   256 pp, 198mm×129mm

ARK PAPERBACKS

THE FEAR OF FREEDOM

Does modern man really want freedom — or are we intrinsically afraid of it? In this brilliant account, Erich Fromm asks the fundamental question — is the fear of freedom the root of the twentieth century's predilection for one or other kind of totalitarianism? The rise of democracy, while setting men free, also created a society where man feels isolated from his fellows, where relationships are impersonal and where insecurity replaces a sense of belonging. This sense of isolation drives man to a devotion and submission to all-powerful organization from the state.

The work, which is both psychoanalytical and historical, is a fundamental interpretation of our age and its problems.

ERICH FROMM

Erich Fromm studied at the universities of Heidelberg, Frankfurt and Munich and was trained in psychoanalysis at the Psychoanalytical Institute in Berlin. All his life he devoted himself to both practical psychological consultancy and theoretical investigation. His many published works have been both influential and illuminating. He died in 1980.

ISBN 0-7448-0014-5   272 pp, 198mm×129mm

ARK PAPERBACKS

PURITY AND DANGER

This remarkable book, which is written in a very graceful, lucid and polemical style, is a symbolic interpretation of the rules of purity and pollution. Mary Douglas shows that to examine what is considered as unclean in any culture is to take a looking-glass approach to the ordered patterning which that culture strives to establish. Such an approach affords a universal understanding of the rules of purity which applies equally to secular and religious life and equally to primitive and modern societies.

MARY DOUGLAS

Mary Douglas is a distinguished international anthropologist who is currently Professor of Anthropology at Northwestern University, Illinois.

ISBN 0-7448-0011-0   208 pp, 198mm×129mm

ARK PAPERBACKS

DICTIONARY OF MODERN CULTURE

With over 300 entries from more than 200 contributors, this is the most comprehensive and informative survey of twentieth century ideas ever published. You will refer to this dictionary time and time again, not only for information and facts, but for stimulation and enjoyment. From Freud to R D Laing, from Proust to Garcia Marquez, from Picasso to Warhol, from Chaplin to Godard, from Debussy to Stockhausen, from Shaw to Pinter, from Wittgenstein to Popper, from Durkheim to McLuhan, from Yeats to Ginsberg, from Wells to Castaneda.

JUSTIN WINTLE

Justin Wintle was educated at Stowe and Magdalen College Oxford, where he graduated in Modern History. He has worked as a freelance writer and editor in London, New York and the Far East. His books include *The Dictionary of Biographical Quotation, Makers of Nineteenth Century Culture* and *The Dragon's Almanac*.

ISBN 0-7448-0007-2   480 pp, 198mm×129mm